A History of
The London Gazette
1665–1965

P. M. HANDOVER

LONDON
HER MAJESTY'S STATIONERY OFFICE
1965

© *Crown copyright 1965*
Published by
HER MAJESTY'S STATIONERY OFFICE
To be purchased from
49 High Holborn, London w.c.1
423 Oxford Street, London w.1
13A Castle Street, Edinburgh 2
109 St. Mary Street, Cardiff
39 King Street, Manchester 2
50 Fairfax Street, Bristol 1
35 Smallbrook, Ringway, Birmingham 5
80 Chichester Street, Belfast 1
or through any bookseller

Printed in England for Her Majesty's Stationery Office
by The Curwen Press, Plaistow, London, E.13

Preface

In November 1965 the *London Gazette* is three hundred years old and it is appropriate that this, the first official history, should be published at this point in time. Through three centuries of this country's history—through the Glorious Revolution of 1688, the Whig settlement, the industrial revolution, the American war of independence, the Napoleonic wars, the Hungry Forties and two Great Wars—the *Gazette* has appeared sometimes daily, sometimes weekly, sometimes twice or thrice weekly, but always faithfully to the preordained pattern, even on Christmas Day and Good Friday when these have been days appointed for publication.

Its very existence today must prompt the question: what kind of newspaper can this be which has so long survived and maintained its usefulness—so much longer than any other British newspaper? Miss Handover has brought a scholarly and sympathetic mind to bear on the long history of the *Gazette*, and from her account emerges a picture of a newspaper created and modified in the course of time to meet persistent, if changing, political and administrative needs.

In the beginning it met the need for authoritative news and in this served the Crown and the Executive. It originally enjoyed a monopoly of the news, but it is interesting that at no time did it consciously attempt to mould public opinion by partisan methods, though the very existence of its monopoly clearly made it a powerful opinion-former. It had incomparable sources of information from overseas. In peace its "foreign correspondents" were the British embassies abroad; in time of war the British generals themselves. The first news of Wellington's victory at Waterloo was inevitably carried in the *Gazette,* and when the newly founded *Times* stopped its presses to carry the news of this famous feat of arms it was the despatch which had been published as a *Gazette* Extraordinary which it printed in full.

The present-day form of a gazette containing governmental announcements and legal notices gradually evolved during the nineteenth century. Today it is a newspaper only in a very specialized sense, but its role in publishing official information is a significant one; for these are still facts which contribute to providing "Information for the People"—the primary aim of the *Gazette* since its inception, whether these be proclamations of the accession of sovereigns, Orders in Council, or even the announcement of premium bond prizes, published in the 1960s as were State Lottery results in the 1690s.

Though the imposing, if not chilling legend "Published by Authority" which it has always borne may be no more than a relic of the ancient Licensing Acts, those words have come through the processes of time to acquire another significance, for it is now indeed a uniquely authoritative journal and it may even be that in another three hundred years historians will still be turning to its pages for reflections of our present age and evidence of the continuity of our political and administrative institutions.

Percy Faulkner

CONTROLLER OF HER MAJESTY'S STATIONERY OFFICE
AND EDITOR OF THE LONDON GAZETTE
AUGUST 1965

Contents

INTRODUCTION
News and Power   2
The Manuscript Newsletter   2
News "For Information of the People"   3
The Restoration   4
A Monopoly of News   5
The Under-Secretary and the Journalist   6
Contemporary Official Newspapers   7

CHAPTER I   1665–70
The *Oxford Gazette*   9
A Distinctive Newspaper Typography   10
Contents of the *Oxford Gazette*   11
The Transfer of the Privilege   13
The Beginning of the *London Gazette*   13
A Rival Authorized Newspaper   14
Survival of the *Gazette*   15

CHAPTER II   1670–84
Robert Yard   19
Money Matters   19
Prerogative and Propaganda   21

CHAPTER III   1684–1702
Changing Contents of the *Gazette*   25

v

James Vernon   26
Public Finance and the *Gazette*   27
The Rise of Professional Journalism   29

CHAPTER IV   1702–10
A Daily Newspaper   33
Harleian Policy   34
De Fonvive of the *Post Man*   35
The Gazetteer's Difficulties   36
The Tonsons Print the *Gazette*   37
Captain Steele becomes Gazetteer   38
Steele's Friends   39
Steele Dismissed   41

CHAPTER V   1710–27
Swift and the *Gazette*   43
The Editorial Burden   44
The Newspaper Stamp Duty   46
Charles Ford   47
The Whigs Take Over the *Gazette*   47

CHAPTER VI   1727–1828
Sir Robert Walpole   53
The Patent Returns to the Under-Secretary   54
Wilkes and "Liberty"   56
"The Only Paper of Authority"   57
The Heyday of Press "Management"   58
The Reform of the Public Service   60
Perquisites and the *Gazette*   61
The *Sun* and the *True Briton*   62
The Times becomes Independent   63
The "New Establishment"   65

CHAPTER VII 1828–45
Paper War for Patronage 67
Palmerston and the *Gazette* 68
Perquisites in 1836 70
John Ramsay McCulloch 71

CHAPTER VIII 1847–67
The Stationery Office Investigates the *Gazette* 73
A Proposal to Amalgamate the Official *Gazettes* 75
The Selling Price is Lowered 76
The Crimean War 77
Company Law 79
"The Chief Work . . . of the *Gazette* Office" 80

CHAPTER IX 1868–1910
Treasury Intervention 81
Thomas Digby Pigott 83
The Editor Dropped 84
Statutory Publicity 85
The "New Establishment" of 1910 88

CHAPTER X 1910–65
The Effects of War 89
The Stationery Office begins to Print 91
The "Prime Source" of State Intelligence 93
The Modern Role of the *Gazette* 94

Introduction

The transcendent secular symbol in our national life has been the Crown, potent through troubled centuries, consecrated at Winchester, beset at Athelney, faltering in Ethelbert, sturdy in Egbert. The hand death lays on kings does not touch the Crown. Only once has it been challenged and although Cromwell put the bauble from him he did not deny that blood and state have substance. That bauble is fount of justice, commissioning power, civil and military, intermediary of foreign relations and inspiration of ultimate sacrifice. By one symbol a Church, a Nation, an Empire and a Commonwealth have been held in allegiance.

At coronation hereditary, conventional, customary, almost mystic and inadequately defined powers are conferred. Most of the roughness of the island story has sprung from the abrasion of those prerogative powers against class and sectional interest, party and popular demand. The twentieth century finds the monarch almost completely withdrawn from active personal government, yet the symbol retains penetrating force. We stroll over broad Crown lands, are defended by the Royal Navy and Air Force and many royal regiments, sue before H.M. judges, are punished in H.M. prisons and live in a style regulated by H.M. Treasury. Posts travel O.H.M.S., ambassadors represent Britannic majesty, institutions of professional men have royal charters. The record of the Crown's dealings has since 1665 been chiefly kept by the official newspaper, the *London Gazette*.

News and Power

Although the genesis of the *London Gazette* was the ambition of a subject the basis was the prerogative power over the dissemination of news. National efficiency depends upon the intelligence received by the Crown. To what degree that information is dispersed is another matter. The wisdom of statesmen is to be secret. In political life the race is to the best-informed but the possession of news is the key to political and international power only so long as it is in private keeping. The printing press, made capable of rapid multiplication in the fifteenth century, enabled news to be widely circulated. In sixteenth-century England the most powerful servants of the Crown, the Cecils, one Lord Treasurer, one Principal Secretary of State, were the most active newsgatherers the country had known but the least disposed to favour its publication. Their release of news even to colleagues was calculated for they feared to weaken their own positions.

Reckless publication might in the same way endanger the supremacy of the Crown. The prerogative court of Star Chamber prohibited the printing of all news except of events abroad and natural disasters, royal declarations and sensational crime at home. This embargo continued until 1640. It delayed the development of newspapers in England since publication was spasmodic when material was irregularly received and in scanty supply.

The Manuscript Newsletter

The Crown only controlled the printing of news. What the pedlar could tell was news in country districts and men higher in the social scale secured the news necessary to them by employing an agent as correspondent or by subscribing to a service of news-letters compiled in London or abroad. The gathering of news for private persons was well established by the sixteenth century. Letters, not being printed, could be varied in content to suit a subscriber's needs: a character in Ben Jonson's *News from the New World* (1620) had from the professional writers "my puritan news, my protestant news, and my pontifical news". Because those served were private and paying customers the contents were, so far as possible, accurate, inclusive and without bias. Propaganda cannot usefully be directed at a solitary reader.

In 1641 Parliament opened the attack on the prerogative by clipping the control of news publication. The genuine thirst of the middling income classes for news was slaked by the printers. The Royalists had a substantial Press. The other side, reflecting the strains between Presbyterian and Independent, soldier and sectarian, was equally riddled with bias. To all the publication of news was subordinate to what it could be argued to prove. As Parliament arrogated the prerogatives of the Crown it was alarmed at the growth of the partisan news publications. A censorship of news publication was introduced in 1643, and later and more stringent Acts established a licensing system.

News "For Information of the People"

Yet Parliament, weaker than the Crown because it rested on electoral sanction, could not resist the demand for news and certain publications were therefore officially allowed. The most important was *Mercurius Politicus*, founded in 1650. Its editor was a journalist, Marchmont Nedham, who during the early summer of that year submitted to the Council of State, then the executive power, a prospectus for a weekly news publication written "in defense of the Commonwealth and for Information of the People", a combination of aims that was then understood to be the legitimate function of news publishing.*

The first number of *Mercurius Politicus* was published on June 13 1650 and it ran for more than 500 weekly numbers, the

*Joseph Frank: *The Beginnings of the English Newspaper 1620–1660* (Harvard 1961); J. B. Williams: *A History of English Journalism to the Foundation of The Gazette* (1908); J. M. French (Editor): *The Life Records of John Milton* (1949–58, 5 vols.). [Books are published in London unless another place is given.]

longest run of any Interregnum news publication. John Milton was the first censor, followed by John Thurloe, who in 1652 was appointed secretary to the Council of State. Thurloe soon accumulated the crucial government departments to his charge, that of intelligence, set up by the Council in 1649, and that of the posts, inland and foreign. Thus astride the channels of communication he made Cromwell, who became Lord Protector in 1655, the best-informed ruler in Europe and himself indispensable to the executive. The news released from Thurloe was Nedham's principal material, although to official matter and parliamentary proceedings he added items supplied by correspondents of his own.

Until the spring of 1660 Nedham more or less continuously survived the changes of administration as editor of the official news—his *Politicus* on Thursdays being supplemented by his *Publick Intelligencer* on Mondays—both bearing under the title the legend "Published by Order of Parliament". Towards the end of 1659 General Monck, planning bloodlessly to restore the King, set up his own news publications, edited by Henry Muddiman, who like Nedham was a schoolmaster turned journalist. Muddiman's papers were the *Parliamentary Intelligencer* and *Mercurius Publicus*, both without sanction other than that of their patron. When the Long Parliament dissolved in March 1660 and Monck's Council of State assumed power pending the King's return, the *Parliamentary Intelligencer* (March 23–April 2) was marked "Published by Order of the Council of State". On the Restoration Muddiman was attached to the office of Charles II's senior Secretary of State, and his journals bore the legend "Published by Order".

The Restoration
Before the Interregnum English monarchs had governed through a Privy Council which by Charles' reign was too swollen with minor household officials to be efficient. He bypassed it through

direct consultation with his chief public servants, the Secretaries of State and others, and the Council was supplanted except on formal occasions. Concurrently its clerks, who in Tudor times had borne much of the routine work of government, were overshadowed by clerks employed by individual ministers. Charles had two Secretaries of State, one being responsible for foreign relations with Protestant countries and the other for the Catholic powers, a division only theoretically observed but the origin of the terms Northern and Southern for their Departments.

Muddiman was to organize the correspondence of both Departments and so had unrivalled access to news. He had as well a valuable perquisite, free postage for the incoming and outgoing posts, which he exploited by setting up a service of manuscript newsletters for private subscribers. The discipline of this service, with its obligations of accuracy, inclusiveness and avoidance of controversy, was congenial to him, more so than it would have been to Nedham who was pre-eminently a partisan writer, and the same qualities were reflected in Muddiman's news publications. In January 1661 his *Parliamentary Intelligencer* was retitled the *Kingdom's Intelligencer*—Charles was no lover of a Parliament—still published "by Order", and a French version prepared by a colleague was circulated with official approval in Holland and France as *Nouvelles Ordinaires de Londres*. Nedham's *Politicus* had similarly appeared in a French version.

A Monopoly of News

The influence of the Interregnum's publishing policy was strong and its Printing Acts were reaffirmed by that of June 1662* which retained the licensing system and laid on the Secretaries the responsibility for scrutinizing matter on affairs of state. They were assisted by a Surveyor of the Press, a new post to which Sir Roger L'Estrange was appointed, his duty being to search out unlicensed printing. A voluble, overbearing man, L'Estrange's ardour

*13 and 14th Car. II c. 33.

deserved reward by 1663 and he was granted by the King a monopoly of news publishing. Muddiman, who thereby lost his *Kingdom's Intelligencer* and *Mercurius Publicus*, agreed to help the journalistically unqualified L'Estrange. By this co-operation he preserved his access to news and could enclose his newsletters with the official journals. These became in August the *Intelligencer* and the *News*.

L'Estrange received his material from the Secretary for the Southern Department, Lord Arlington, through Arlington's under-secretary, Joseph Williamson. This post, hitherto little more than a clerkship, Williamson was manipulating through his employer's indolence into one of power. For years he subordinated to his work every outside interest except a love of music. In him an intelligence and scholarship much respected at Oxford were coupled with a hoarding instinct that drove him to amass portable objects, and similarly he amassed information. He divined that Muddiman's virtual control of news could be of utmost value to his own career and he greedily envied Muddiman's profits from the newsletter service. It became imperative to him to supersede Muddiman while retaining his professional help. In Williamson's plan to realize this purpose the *London Gazette* had its beginning.

The Under-Secretary and the Journalist

The financial success of Muddiman's newsletter service depended on the free postage for the letters directed to him from the gentlemen and tradesmen and officials in the provinces who acted as his reporters. Without their assistance he would have had little home news for neither the Secretaries nor any other minister had responsibility for home affairs except in times of stress or danger. All Muddiman's letters had however to pass through the head "Letter Office of England", the forerunner of the General Post Office. Williamson planned to filch the addresses and set up his own service. He had also to circumvent L'Estrange's monopoly.

During the summer of 1665 when the plague ravaged London the Court retired to Oxford although L'Estrange remained in the capital to publish his *Intelligencer* and *News*. Bereft of Muddiman, who had gone with the Secretaries and the Court, his journals, the only source of printed news available, were pathetic publications, their scanty material fattened out by large type and plenty of white space. Obvious incompetence gave Williamson the opening. It was plain, he intimated to L'Estrange, that the latter's distance from the Secretaries hampered the proper execution of his duties: the moment might be convenient for the monopoly to be relinquished in return for a pension of £100.*

As for Muddiman, he was captured by Williamson as the first editor of a new official journal, an arrangement attractive to him since he would be able to enclose his manuscript letters as before —indeed, this was essential to Williamson's plan. No great preparation was needed for Muddiman's organization was in being and Oxford possessed a printing house capable of the work. Williamson disregarded the protests of L'Estrange, warned the Letter Office to watch Muddiman's correspondence, and set to work with the journalist on number 1 of the *Oxford Gazette*, "Published by Authority", on November 16 1665.†

Contemporary Official Newspapers
There were two powerful influences on Williamson when he planned the *Gazette*. The first was the example of Thurloe and

---

*Williamson, in Arlington's name, to L'Estrange, October 15 1665. For a discussion of this letter, summarized in the Calendar of State Papers Domestic (C.S.P.D.) 1665–66 and discussed in the preface, see J. G. Muddiman: *The King's Journalist* (1923), p. 174.

†Number 1 was not dated, number 2 was "*From* Thursday, November 16 *to* Monday, November 20 1665". Monday and Thursday were thereafter the publication days—as they had been of Nedham's journals because of the posts—and the dates of items fit with a Monday, November 13 to Thursday, November 16 publication date for number 1. The copy in the library of the Controller of the Stationery Office is dated in a contemporary hand November 13, but, an item from Oxford being November 14, this must refer to the first part of the double date.

Nedham and the official news publications of the Interregnum. The second was the official Press abroad. One of Europe's chief newspapers was the *Amsterdam Gazette*, which had taken that name in 1662 although it had been founded in 1618 as the *Courante uyt Italien, Duytslandt, etc.* This *Courante* was the first regularly appearing sheet of news in Europe and an English translation was briefly available in London in 1620 and 1621.

There was similarly a French translation of the *Courante* in Paris and this led in 1631 to the foundation of the *Gazette de Paris*, edited successively by Théophraste Rénaudot, a protégé of Cardinal Richelieu, and by his son the Abbé Rénaudot. In Williamson's time these two *Gazettes* were celebrated all over Europe and owing to the importance to England of her principal rivals, France and Holland, were familiar in London. The Paris *Gazette* was published under a royal privilege of 1631 and like its contemporary of Amsterdam contained news from official sources at a period when Louis XIV's organization of the French civil service was the admiration of the neighbours of France.*

*The English version of the *Courante* is discussed by Stanley Morison in his lecture "The Origins of the Newspaper", privately printed (1954). The French *Gazette* and its contemporaries are discussed in "Les Débuts de la Presse française, nouveaux aperçus" in *Acta Bibliothecae Gotoburgensis*, 1951, iv, by Folke Dahl, Fanny Petibon and Marguerite Boulet, and *Histoire de la Presse française* by René de Livran (Lausanne 1965).

Chapter I 1665–70

The Oxford Gazette

The most convincing derivation of the term gazette is from gaza, the Greek word for a treasury or store. It was in use in Italy during the sixteenth century where to the banking houses that financed European trade and warfare the professional compilations of news would be treasuries. The Italian gazettes, both as written newsletters and printed, were being circulated to statesmen throughout Europe by the end of the century.

A variety of terms, usually Italian in origin, was adopted for printed news as its production spread through Europe. In London during the 1620s the bookseller would be asked for the latest coranto, anglicized as currant, and in the 1640s the term mercury (cf. *Mercurius Politicus*) gained ground. In this country a gazette was generally understood to mean manuscript news: despite the example of France none of the many Interregnum news publications had been called a gazette. Thus Williamson and Muddiman chose for the title of their official newspaper a term that was to English ears unhackneyed and, because of the official contemporaries abroad and the prized manuscript service, had implications of authority and accuracy.

The *Oxford Gazette* was printed by Leonard Lichfield. There was in 1665 no University Press at Oxford but like Cambridge the University was exempt from regulations that had confined the printing trade to London. The privilege to print was assigned by the University to selected printers, Lichfield having been appointed in 1657 in succession to his father. When the Court of

Charles I retired to Oxford during the civil war it was Lichfield senior who had done the royal printing, substituting for the King's Printers, appointed by royal patent, whose house was in London.

A Distinctive Newspaper Typography

Hitherto the typical English news publication was not a paper but a book or booklet—the term newspaper has been deliberately avoided in this account. Until the civil war the traditional octavo book format with a title page, blank verso and text beginning on page 3 was preserved. The greater activity in news publishing after restrictions were lifted led to a modification of this format, the blank verso being jettisoned and title and text appearing on page 1. Some of these publications might be called newspapers for they are a paper of news, a half sheet folded to make four pages, but Nedham's reverted to the booklet form.

The *Oxford Gazette* was however a true newspaper, a half sheet of paper $11\frac{1}{4} \times 6\frac{3}{4}$ in. printed on both sides. It finally established a distinctive format for news publication. Foreign example had influenced it, for example the 1618 *Courante* of Amsterdam had been a half sheet printed on both sides in two columns, and another influence was Lichfield's bible printing, where the small type customarily used required to be divided into columns.

There was—and still is—much in common between bible and newspaper printing. Both pack much matter as economically as possible by using types of small size; both have long runs. Owing to the regulation of the printing trade few printers in the seventeenth century were equipped for such work. The bible might only be printed by the King's Printers and by the Universities of Oxford and Cambridge. After the Restoration the King's Printers—there were two sharing the patent—could not themselves print and leased the right to professionals, one of whom, Thomas Newcomb, was the printer of the London edition of the *Oxford Gazette*.*

The first number of this London edition which, according to the imprint, was done "for the use of some merchants and gentlemen", probably appeared some days after number 1 had been printed at Oxford, for Samuel Pepys the diarist only saw a copy on November 22. Thereafter it was concurrent with the Oxford edition, appearing on the same days, Mondays and Thursdays. Both editions were in the same format. The column width of early numbers showed slight variation according to the amount of matter but after number 15, when Newcomb changed the broad bourgeois (*c.* 9-point) to a narrower version familiar in bible printing it was stable at about 17 picas. Column width was a detail: it was the adoption by the *Gazette* of the two-column half sheet that was the beginning of the multicolumn typography typical of the world's newspapers today.†

Contents of the Oxford Gazette

Muddiman concentrated on two main categories of news: the foreign reports and those from the English havens on shipping movements. These two categories dominated every issue during his editorship. The minor items, such as the weekly bills of

*Newcomb had been the printer of *Mercurius Politicus* for most of its career, of Nedham's other journal and of Muddiman's *Parliamentary Intelligencer*. At the Restoration he became one of the official printers to the House of Commons as well as obtaining the share in the royal patent.

†The heading of the *Gazette* was also an important typographical innovation. Nedham's newsbooks had had long titles (*Mercurius Politicus, comprising the sum of foreign intelligence, with the affairs now on foot in the three nations of England, Scotland, and Ireland, for information of the people*). This took up most of page 1 and was separated from the text by the line "Published by Order of Parliament" above a rule. For the three-word title of the *Gazette* upper and lower-case, not capitals, were used and the type design was new to England, having been introduced by Newcomb and other printers of official documents and announcements. The size was canon (between 42 and 48 point), Oxford having a light version known as French canon, Newcomb a sturdier and larger canon of Dutch origin. Subsequently the short heading in canon was adopted by other London newspapers.

mortality, which included deaths from the plague, amounted to one or two in an issue, and apart from news of the King and Court, were usually legal: lists of circuit judges and sheriffs, occasional reports of crime and its punishment.

More than a dozen English seaports regularly sent news to Muddiman. His correspondents wrote not only of the arrival and departure of the great trading vessels and the prizes, but of the coast-wise traffic which was then the chief carrier of all domestic bulk goods as well as of many travellers. The shipping items in the *Gazette* reflected the preoccupation with trade that in the following century was to make this country the richest in the world. No earlier news publication in London had had this range.

The foreign news was arranged in order of place of origin, the Southern Department countries being placed first—an order that was to leave its mark on English journalism for a hundred years. In the treatment of the items selected from the Secretaries' letters Muddiman was guided by his experience with private subscribers. The news was presented with detachment: there was no comment except on the likelihood of accuracy in a report. He avoided controversial subjects and gossip, disclosed no political sympathy and neither advocated nor dissuaded. The *Gazette* shaped by Muddiman was not partisan. Pepys found it "very pretty, full of news and no folly in it"; by folly he meant editorial comment. Thus, although the *Gazette* was deeply indebted to forerunners and contemporaries, Williamson and Muddiman, Lichfield and Newcomb, had produced a professional newspaper that combined innovation with tradition.

Nedham's basis, news for the "information of the people", was broader than Muddiman's. From the beginning the readership of the *Gazette* was not the general public but the mercantile classes, the legal profession, municipal officers and officials serving at home and abroad.

Numb. 570.

Mercurius Politicus

COMPRISING

The ſum of Foreign Intelligence, with the Affairs now on foot in the Three Nations

OF

ENGLAND, *SCOTLAND*, & *IRELAND*.

For Information of the People.

Publiſhed by Authority.

From Thurſday *June* 2. *to* Thurſday *June* 9. 1659.

From Dunkirk, June 5. *S. N.*

Ur men here, and at *Mardike*, are well reſolved touching the late alteration made in *England*, and ready to ſerve the Parliament in the defence of theſe places, to the utmoſt hazard of their lives, as they at large ſignified to our Governer *Lockhart* before his embarkment for *England*. The Engliſh Regiments are ſtill at *Amiens*, the French under Marſhal *Turcine* lie part of them thereabout, ready for any occaſion : The Spaniſh Troops alſo appear in a body, but all is quiet, and we yet partake of the benefit of the Ceſſation of,

8 N

The Oxford Gazette.

Published by Authority.

Oxon. Nov. 7.

This day the Reverend Dr. *Walter Blandford*, Warden of *Wadham Colledge* in this University, was elected Ld. Bishop of this See, vacant by the death of Dr. *Paul*, late Bishop here.

Oxon. Nov. 12. This Day His Majesty in Council according to the usual custom, having the Roll of Sheriffs presented to him, pricked these Persons following to be Sheriffs for the succeeding Year, in their respective Counties of *England* and *Wales.*

Berks.	Basil Brent, *Esquire.*
Bedford.	Thot Snagge, *Esq.*
Buckingham.	Symon Bennet, *Esq.*
Cumberland.	Sir William Dalston, *Baronet.*
Chester.	Sir Iohn Arderne, *Knight.*
Cambridge.	Sir Tho: Willis, *Kt. and Baronet.*
Cornwal.	Thot Dorrel, *Esq.*
Devon.	Iohn Kelland, *Esq.*
Dorset.	Roger Clavel, *Esq.*
Derby.	Sir Samuel Sleigh, *Knight.*
Yorkshire.	Sir Francis Cobb, *Knight.*
Essex.	Sir Heneage Fetherston, *Baronet.*
Glocester.	Sir Richard Cox, *Baronet.*
Hertford.	Sir Ionathan Keat, *Baronet.*
Hereford.	Tho: Rod, *Esq.*
Kent.	Sir Humphry Miller, *Baronet.*
Lancaster.	William Spencer, *Esq.*
Leicester.	Sir Edward Smith, *Baronet.*
Lincoln.	Sir Iohn Brownlow, *Kt. and Baronet.*
Monmouth.	Walter Morgan, *of Landillo Patholly, Esq.*
Northumberland.	William Middleton, *Esq.*
Northampton.	Ioseph Hanbury, *Esq.*
Norfolk.	Sir Iohn Hobard, *Baronet.*
Nottingham.	Iohn White of Cotgrave, *Esq.*
Oxford.	Thot Wheate of Glymston, *Esq.*
Rutland.	Charles Halford, *Esq.*
Shropshire.	Sir Humphr Beggs.
Somerset.	•Sir Hugh Smith, *Baronet.*
Stafford.	Frant: Leveson, *alias* Fowler, *Esq.*
Suffolk.	Sir Edmond Bacon, *Baronet.*
Southampton.	Thot Neale, *Esq.*
Surrey.	Sir Iohn Evelyn, *Baronet.*
Sussex.	Robert Fowle, *Esq.*
Warwick.	Charles Bentley, *Esq.*
Worcester.	Sir William Cookes of Norgrave, *Kt.*
Wilts.	Sir Iohn Weld, *Knight.*
Anglesey.	Rowland Buildey, *Esq.*
Brecknock.	Hugh Powel, *Esq.*
Cardigan.	Iames Stedman. *Esq.*
Carnarvon.	Tho: Maderne, *Esq.*
Denbigh.	Sir Charles Goodman.
Flint.	Sir Roger Mostlyn.
Glamorgan.	William Basset of Brabskin, *Esq.*
Merioneth.	Lewis Lloyd, *Esq.*
Montgomry.	•Ed: Kynaston, *Esq.*
Pembroke.	Sir Herbert Perrot.
Radnor.	Nicht Taylor, *Esq.*
Carmarthen.	William Lloyd, *Esq.*

Paris, Nov. 14. Monsieur *de Turenne* is not yet returned, but expected here every day. Most of the Gentry of *Nivernois* & *Auvergne* are said to have withdrawn themselves, and got into a place of strength; one Mon-

sieur *de Camillac* having been put to death by the Commissioners of the *Grands Iours* : It seems they had laid some new Taxes or Impositions on those parts : There are Troups marching against them , and it is thought they will soon be reduced . My Lord *Aubigny* Lord *Almoner* to her Majesty , having layen sick some time here of an Hydropsie attended with a Flux, is this week dead.

Paris Novemb: 18. The *Mareschal de Turenne* arrived here on Sunday last from the Frontiers , whence he brings account that the Succors intended against the Prince of *Munster* had passed in small parties, and that they had been received at *Miestricht* by *Monsieur Beverng* in the name of the States General.

Guernzy, Octob. 30. Yesterday came into our Road the *Unity* Frigot , Captain *Trafford* Commander, who brought in a Prize Captain *Iohn Gitson* of *Flushing*, being a Privateer of 7 Guns, and 45. Men.

Chattham Nov. 14. Captain *Elliot* Commander of the *Saphire* has taken 3 Busses, two of them out of 50 at the *Dogger-sands*, under the Protection of four of their Men of War. In his passage home, tis said, he saw several tops of Ships, Masts, &c. which seemed to be the effects of some Wreck , which God be thanked we doe not heare to have been any of the *English* Ships.

Oxon: Novemb: 12. Not knowing what accompt the Publick has hitherto received of the Progress of the Prince of *Munster's* Armes , we have thought it not improper without further repetition, to give an account of such places as he at present stands possest of in the Enemies Country viz : The Castle and Territory of *Borclo,* (being of right his own,) and for many yeares unjustly detained from him) the Castle of *Litchteavorde* and the Towns of *Lochem* , *Dotechem*, *Diepenheim*, *Goer*, *Enschede, Oldeasel, Othmarschen* , *Hardesbreg, Ommen, Wildenberg, Keppel, Almeloe, Hengel, Gramsberg,* and *Vennebrug* , and now more lately *Winschot* with the Fort of *Bragges Scanz*, the Castle of *Wedde,* and the Cloyster of *Appel,* out of which a party of his had some time before been forced by the *Hollanders.* And it is confirmed to us by several good hands from *Brussels* , that he has taken the strong Fort of *Bourtaing,* and *Reid,* a Sea-port scituate near *Damme* and *Delps* Isle , in diverse of which places His Highness has left very considerable Garrisons , besides his Feild-Army, which consists of 18000 Foot , and 6000 Horse effective.

Deale, Novemb. 8. The wind, since my last continues very high, but I hear of no harm done yet. The *Phœnix* hath brought in a Prize here.

Norwich Novemb: 8. I lately received from a good hand in *Rochel* dated *Octob:* 28, a short account of the taking the Island St. *Ustache* , which for the manner of the attempt, may not be unworthy the communication ; it was brought by a *French* *West-India* ship which came from St. *Christophers* about 3 leagues from it, and runs thus, That on the 12 of *August* about 300 of the Forces belonging to *Jamaica* went thither with a resolution of an attaque . There is but one landing place in the whole Island, and that of such difficult access, that but 2 at most can go abrest , up an ascent to an eminent place, in the top of which was a strong Fort, which on this occasion had been well furnished with powder and Guns left by *De Ruiter* and mand with 450 Soldiers, who were nevertheless so surprised at the boldness of the Undertaking, that they delivered themselves up with very little resistance.

Plymouth. Nov. 5. The Weather of late hath been

A   very

very tempestuous on these Coasts, and we hear that a Dutch man or *Hamburger* (uncertain yet whether) hath been cast away at the Barre. A ship from *Virginia* belonging to *London* was cast away about 3 Leagues from this place, and 5 men lost; and another *Virginia* ship driven a shore but got off without much damage.

Chester, Nov. 11. This City and Country, (thanks be to God) remain in good health, without the least Infection. We have advice from *Duncanon* in *Ireland*, That the Governor, Sir *Nicholas Armorer* hath secured a Ship bound from *Guinee*, worth in Gold dust, and other rich Commodities, 5000 *l.* which by storm was forced into that River. The Particulars what she is, whither bound, and upon whose account, is not yet said. The Winds have been so cross here, that five *Irish* Pacquets are said to be still detained at *Holy-Head*, where of late there fell a Storm of Hail, so great, that some affirm, several grains were taken up, which were four inches about.

Southwould. Novemb. 11. Yesternight came by this Town a Fleet of loaden Colliers; about 30 Sail of great Shipps and many small Vessels were in sight before night: what passed afterward we know not; 'tis hoped this night or to morrow morning they will be in the River of *Thames*.

Falmouth Novemb. 3. A small Vessel of *Apsom* was cast away on this Coast, loaden with Oranges and Lemmons, but the men were saved.

Hull Novemb: 10. This day arrived several Ships from *New-Castle* and *Scarborough*, which assur'd us that Coast is all clear. This day sailed his Majesties Ship the *Bath*, and in her Convoy three Ships for *Yarmouth Peere*, as also the Victualling Shipps and Hoy laden with Timber for the use of the Navy.

Dublin. Novemb. 4th. The House of Commons expressing their just resentment that some Persons who had the Honor of being Members of that House, and consequently were admitted to consult of the weighty affairs of the Kingdom, should be so far debauch'd from their duty, as Traiterously to conspire against the Government, and joyn themselves in raising a Rebellion particularly design'd on the 21 of *May*, 1663. did on the 2d instant (the first time of their meeting by reason of the several necessary Prorogations) by Declaration testifie their just Detestation and Abhorrence of that Traiterous Engagement, & that though many other weighty Affaires were at present before them, they would in the first place enter upon the consideration of that particular, returning their most humble and hearty thanks to his Grace the Lord Lieutenant, whose singular prudence and circumspection had prevented its progress, and assuring him of their constant Loyalty to his Majestie, and their obedience to him as their Governour; This declaration was presented to the Lord Lieutenant by their Speaker, and in consequence of it, they pass this Vote;

Novemb: 4th 1664. Whereas several Members of this House (viz:) *Robert Shapcote, John Chambers, Thomas Boyd, Alexander Staples, Abel Warren, John Ruxton,* and *Thomas Scot* Esquires, had been by Vote of this House suspended from sitting in the House until the farther pleasure of the House be known; And to the end it may be accordingly signified, Ordered upon the Question, that this House doe appoint Thursday morning next at 10 of the clock, to hear all and every the said Persons that have any defence to make for themselves against the Charge of Treason whereof they are accused, otherwise this House will then proceed to give Judgment upon the Evidence now before them.

Oxon. 13. Nov. This Morning arrived here from *Tangier*, Major *Palmes Fairbose*, Major of Colonel *Norwoods* Regiment in that Garrison, who parted from thence the 16th past, and arrived at *Calais* in 15 days, where he was kept by the violent cross Weather nine days for a Passage. By him we have a particular account of the prosperous condition of that Place, and of the great care and industry of the Lord *Bellasis*, his Majesties Governor there, in providing this important Place with all necessaries that may render it in this conjuncture as well secure to it self, as of protection and defence to the Shipping of this Nation, in their Passage to and from the *Straights*, of which the following Relation brought by the same hands, gives us an eminent instance: Upon the 13th past, it happened that certain Victuallers, intended for *Tangier*, under the Convoy of the *Merlin* Frigot of 12 Guns, Captain *Haward* Commander, (the same that some Moneths since, in a small West-country Vessel with 8 men and a boy, so bravely mastered the Turks Man of War) to whom several Merchants Ships to the number of 16 or 17, had joyned themselves, parting with the *Fox* Frigot and a Merchant-man, bound for *Sally*, on a particular design, and at the expence of a private Merchant, off of *Cape Spurts*, The Merchant-men (as their custom is) saluting those two at their going off for *Salley*, gave notice to Five *Dutch* Men of War already under Sail before the Bay of *Cadiz*, the Admiral of 56. Guns, one of 45, one of 40, and two of 36. each, who having the Wind at N. W. were presently up with ours. The *Merlin* was the headmost, & perceived not the *Dutch*, who came in the stern (it seems) till they had possessed themselves of two Victuallers, and one Merchant-man bound for *Legorn*, Capt. *Allen* Commander. He immediately tacked about; and so mawled them for four hours, that our whole Fleet had time to escape into the Bay of *Tangier*. Having received several shots under Water, his masts and tackling much maimed; and perceiving the headmost of the *Dutch* ships, the *Charles*, a Ship of 45 Guns, who had done him the most mischief, to be making after our Fleet, and that she would inevitably take them all, he frankly run himself aboard her, where he fought a full hour board and board: Till at length the Captain being shot through the shoulder with one Musket bullet, and grazed from the fore-head with another, having now seen all his Men, save 10, fall dead, or desperately wounded by his side, He was at last brought to yield, and was carryed into *Cadiz*, where he is said to be in a hopeful way of recovery.

The *Dutch* are said to have pursued our Merchants up to the very Mould of *Tangier*, whence, by the Fire of the great Battery, and of the Musketeers the Lord *Bellasis* had very seasonably disposed there, they were beat off, and the Fleet of Merchants preserved, riding in defiance of them. The *Tunis* Merchant, a Ship of 28. Guns, behaved her self very well in this occasion, and so galled the *Dutch* at the former part of the Action, that they confest they were upon the point once of quitting the *Merlin*.

Oxon: Novemb: 14. The *Flanders* and *Holland* Males having miss'd us for several Posts together by reason of the cross winds as is supposed, we have no late news from those parts: Only it is assured by the Letters, from *Paris* 8 instant, that General *Gorgas* has certainly gained a Passage upon the *Hollanders*, wherby he has freed those 5000 of the Prince of *Munster's* men which were said to be shut up near *Winschoten* by Prince *Maurices* Troups, having kil'd the greatest part of those that were set to maintain the Post, and taken five peice of Cannon. Those Letters say farther that the States of the Province of *Holland* were so netled at the Printing the Proposition of the Province of *Overysel* concerning the re-establishment of the Prince of *Orange*, that they ordered it forthwith to be supprest, and fell upon debate whether a Proclamation should not be issued for prohibiting the like Addresses for the future, but it found such opposition even from *Amsterdam* it selfe, that they were forced to lay it aside. General *Wrangel* is said to have arriv'd 25 past old stile in *Pomer-land*, attended with 3 men of War, and three other Vessels laden with ammunition.

The account of the Weekly Bill at *London*, runs thus,
Total 1359.   Plague 1050.   Decreased 428.

Oxford, Printed by *Leonard Lichfeild*, Printer to the University, 1665.

JOSEPH WILLIAMSON
The founder of the *Oxford Gazette* in 1665.
Reproduced by courtesy of the National Portrait Gallery

JAMES VERNON
Secretary of State 1698–1702.
Reproduced by courtesy of the National Portrait Gallery

RICHARD STEELE
Gazetteer 1707–10.
Reproduced by courtesy of the National Portrait Gallery

JACOB TONSON SENIOR
Printer of the *Gazette* between 1707 and 1711.
Reproduced by courtesy of the National Portrait Gallery

The Transfer of the Privilege

The authority for the publication of the *Oxford Gazette* was ultimately the King, represented by his Secretary of State, Arlington, who under the Printing Act of 1662 licensed matters of state. When on November 28 1665 L'Estrange attempted to compete with the *Gazette* by bringing out *Publick Intelligencer*, he did so under his monopoly and his legend was "with sole privilege". Only one number appeared: he then reverted to his newsbooks, of which nine "with privilege" appeared during December. Having reasserted his monopoly he appealed successfully against its invasion, and was granted £100 a year, a pension to be paid out of the profits of the *Gazette*. The privilege was then transferred to the Secretaries of State.*

Meanwhile relations between Muddiman and Williamson deteriorated rapidly. The secret purpose of employing the newsletter-writer had not been relaxed, and although Muddiman had taken such precautions as having his post sent in bulk parcels, the Letter Office had obtained a number of addresses. Approaches were made by Williamson's agents to Muddiman's subscribers and in disgust the newsletter-writer decided to quit.

The Beginning of the London Gazette

In London the plague was abating. On January 27 1666 the Court returned as far as Hampton Court and Lichfield's connection with the *Oxford Gazette* ceased after no. 21. The last stage of the Court's return to the capital was accomplished on February 1, and no. 24, the issue for February 1–5, was the first to be titled the *London Gazette*, the title it has since consistently borne. The bi-weekly publication on Mondays and Thursdays was continued.

Muddiman edited only two *London Gazettes*, nos. 24 and 25,

*H.M.C., Ormonde MSS, new series, iii, 351. The publications mentioned are to be found in volume 64 of the Burney collection at the British Museum. *Publick Intelligencer* was as close a typographical imitation of the *Gazette* as its far inferior supply of news would permit.

before he attached himself to Sir William Morice, Secretary of State for the Northern Department. On February 7 Charles Perrot of Oriel College, Oxford, and Gray's Inn had an interview with Williamson and accepted the editorship of the *Gazette*.* Perrot was then in his mid-forties. He had travelled to learn foreign languages—an essential qualification for the *Gazette* appointment—and shortly before he was offered the post he had written a couple of pamphlets in defence of the prerogative. He shared with Williamson a love of music and Anthony à Wood, the chronicler of Oxford worthies, credited him with good breeding and "a sweet nature".†

Perrot was an academic writer: he was neither a journalist nor an editor. He lacked lowly talents needed by a reporter, such as scenting out the official possessed of the information, and he failed to organize an efficient substitute for the Secretaries' lack of home news. The "sweet nature" left him submissive to the pushful under-secretary and reluctant to act on his own initiative. Williamson's ambition and curiosity, his love of power and his ceaseless industry, had enabled him rapidly to grasp the techniques of newsgathering and editing and it was he who ran the *Gazette* with Perrot as his tool.‡

A Rival Authorized Newspaper

Muddiman remained his own master. He persuaded Morice§ to exercise the share of L'Estrange's monopoly and on June 4 1666

*C.S.P.D. 1666, p. 232.

†Anthony à Wood, *Athenae Oxonienses* (1848), p. 88, and *The Life and Times of Anthony Wood* (Oxford 1891), p. 273.

‡C.S.P.D., 1669, p. 301, Williamson to Robert Francis, April 29: "Mr Perrot ought to have spoken to Swaddell or someone else to give him an account of the King's movements." C.S.P.D., 1670, p. 106, J. Man of Swansea to Williamson: "I have addressed my correspondence to Chas. Perrot upon three occasions, which might have merited a place in the *Gazette*," C.S.P.D., 1670, p. 40, where Perrot thrust on Williamson the decision to retain a correspondent of proved worth, and C.S.P.D., 1669, p. 274, where Williamson issued precise instructions for an obituary, are other illustrations of Perrot's ineffectiveness.

§Morice was a relative and "elbow counsellor" of Muddiman's former patron Monck, created Duke of Albemarle.

no. 1 of a second official newspaper, *Current Intelligence*, issued from the second Secretary's office. It was published on the same days as the *Gazette*, bore the same legend, "Published by Authority", and was printed by Newcomb's associate John Macock.*

Williamson resented the appearance of a competitor published by authority. In no. 71 of the *Gazette*, July 16–19, the cherished line was given more prominence and weight by being set in the large blackletter or old English type then used for such formal matter as proclamations. The typographical change was promptly imitated in *Current Intelligence*, July 23–26. The *Gazette* countered by changing the small roman of the date line for further blackletter to add to the importance of the heading.†

Survival of the Gazette

That the *Gazette* survived, hampered by an inferior news service and an amateur editor, and burdened by the charge to L'Estrange, testifies to Williamson's determination. He and Perrot were relieved of the competition only by the Great Fire of the first week of September 1666. Macock and Newcomb, who had their printing houses by Baynard's Castle on the perimeter of Blackfriars,‡ were burnt out, but the latter restarted his business in the Savoy and the *Gazette* missed only one issue, reappearing on Monday September 10. *Current Intelligence* was not resumed but Muddiman continued until a few years before his death in 1692 the manuscript service, which was often preferred to the *Gazette*. Williamson adapted his office organization to meet this threat and expanded the manuscript service that he had begun in 1666.

*The typography of the *Gazette* was also closely followed except that in *Current Intelligence* the foreign news was collected under centred headings of countries: ITALY, FRANCE, POLAND etc.

†Burney 66 (British Museum).

‡Newcomb's house was approximately on the present site of the Mermaid Theatre, opposite to the office of *The Times* in Queen Victoria Street.

Muddiman charged £5 a year for the newsletter service. The *Gazette*, like earlier news publications, was financed by revenue from sales, at 1d. a copy. Advertising on the scale of later centuries was impractical since goods were not mass produced, but certain commodities already depended on press advertising. By the summer of 1666 the *Gazette* was being pressed to admit notices of books and medicines, but they were excluded as "not properly the business of a paper of intelligence. . . . We will not charge the *Gazette* with advertisements, unless they be matter of State."* This was Williamson's first view of newspaper finance.

Perrot treated the activities of the King, which were prominent in the home news, with formality. Although the fall of Clarendon, the Lord Chancellor, in the summer of 1667 was a yielding by Charles to the will of Parliament, who held the minister responsible for ill success in the Dutch war, Perrot treated it as an exercise of the prerogative: "August 31. His Majesty having thought fit to take the Great Seal from the Earl of Clarendon, hath this day been pleased to give it to the Honourable Sir Orlando Bridgman." To the initiated the *Gazette* was indispensable for they could read between the lines: upon the clues it offered deductions could be made or conclusions formed.

In the reports of preparations against the Dutch Perrot allowed

---

*No. 62, June 14–18 1666. At the time a separate publication for advertisements was promised. On June 25 1666 L'Estrange issued no. 1 of *Publick Advertisements*, which was to contain insertions inadmissible to the *Gazette*. Only one number appeared and the idea was dormant for nearly a year. In no. 159 of the *Gazette*, May 23–27 1667, the promise of a separate sheet was revived: "Order is taken for the printing of all ordinary advertisements, at the office of the clerk and register of the passes [i.e. passports, a function of the Secretaries], at the Peacock in the Strand."

The publication was the more successful *City Mercury* of Thomas Bromhall. Issues were distributed free but the advertisers paid 2s. 6d. an insertion (S.P.D., Chas. II, 187, no. 265 and vol. 450, no. 92). According to F. S. Siebert, *The Freedom of the Press in England 1476–1776* (Urbana 1952), p. 295, the *City Mercury* ran from June 10 to October 24 1667. Bromhall was related to one of Williamson's clerks, and joined the under-secretary in at least one business deal, so Williamson was in no doubt connected with the venture (C.S.P.D., 1667, April 24, p. 723 and also C.S.P.D., 1669).

expressions of optimism in his correspondents to pass and the severe defeat of the English navy during the Channel battle of June 1667 was toned down.* It was to be one of the handicaps of an editor of the *Gazette* that his opportunities for editing as the term is understood in modern times were negligible. He could do little to check for himself the accuracy of reports or so to arrange material that readers did not have to deduce reality, and he was perpetually inhibited by the reluctance of his official correspondents to permit editorial revision for the press.

That Perrot was not a successful editor was becoming apparent by the end of 1667 when Williamson was told that there was "a general complaint of the *Gazette* wanting domestic intelligence".† It was easier for this to be supplied in the manuscript service as it expanded to meet the competition of Muddiman. By 1670 the number of letters being sent out had reached nearly two hundred and Perrot appears to have been involved with their preparation as well as with the *Gazette*.‡ When a friend of Williamson's wrote in May that "I hope I may hear your Parrott talk once a week", the connection with the

---

*No. 59, June 4–7, admitted that some ships were seriously damaged and that casualties were high. For optimistic reports see e.g. "The fortifications of this town [Plymouth] are very well advanced and the whole country in good posture" in no. 67, June 2–5, and from Dublin, "We are here very vigorously employed in forming our militia, which will be considerable in this town . . . the same care is taken generally throughout the whole kingdom."

†The dearth of home news and the absence of advertising often gave Newcomb space for typographical experiments. In no. 75 a dispatch from Whitehall on the recent sea fight was virtually headlined by being given a heading, set in a large size of italic with "Narrative" in blackletter to give the word prominence—the printers of the seventeenth century having no other bold face. The report from the Dutch Admiral De Ruyter, which appeared in the next number (August 2–6), was similarly treated. Display was used for the names of preachers at Court and for those of circuit judges. These beginnings of a newspaper typography had eventually to be curtailed because of the pressure on space as advertisements were admitted.

‡At 2 a.m. on April 21 1670 the clerk at the Letter Office noted for Williamson that the newsletters had not yet come down from Perrot (C.S.P.D., 1670, p. 174) but in the same month advertisements for the *Gazette* were still being sent to him (ibid, p. 182).

twice-weekly *Gazette* may have been tapering off.* During 1670 the editorial work was transferred to another of Williamson's clerks, Robert Yard, closely supervised by his employer.

*C.S.P.D., 1670, p. 209.

Chapter II 1670-84

Robert Yard

At this period the officers of the Crown worked in the Palace of Whitehall, and Yard's desk was in Arlington's room where he was at hand for copying, translating and making extracts of the correspondence connected with the Secretaryship. He was also responsible for the cupboards and cabinets containing the reference books, maps and papers used by the committee on foreign affairs.* After he became editor of the *Gazette* he found Arlington's own staff took advantage of Williamson's absence to torment him: "I am sure they endeavour all they can to run me into errors", he wrote miserably to Williamson on August 18 1673. Information for the *Gazette* would be withheld and then fault found with it, and the arrangement with Newcomb for printing official documents would also have been invaded but for the printer's loyalty to Williamson.†

Money Matters

Financially the *Gazette* was insignificant. The profits were divided between Arlington and his fellow Secretary to be passed

*Florence M. Evans, *The Principal Secretary of State* (Manchester 1923), p. 163, quotes a letter from Williamson to Arlington, *c.* 1673, describing not only Yard's duties but those of Henry Ball, who conducted the manuscript service from Scotland Yard.

The foreign committee's establishment by Charles, announced in the *Gazette* for February 3–6 1668, was one of the signals of the decay of the Privy Council. It met once a week, on Mondays.

†According to Yard later (Evans, p. 217), a printer would pay £30 or £40 for an official document, such as a treaty, authorized for separate republication.

on to their under-secretaries but Williamson's opposite number declared: "I could never find they amounted to very much." The cost of paper and printing, and the salaries of the writers and translators had to be deducted. There was as well the cost of the *Gazette* in French, the *Gazette de Londres*, produced for circulation abroad following Muddiman's *Nouvelles Ordinaires*. This, according to the under-secretary, "always turned to loss".*

The financial situation could not improve while paid advertising was excluded. In the early years the most frequent departmental advertiser was the Exchequer. After the Restoration Charles was harassed for money and in 1663 an Act (17 Car. II c.1) introduced the numbered tally, the split wooden account sticks being issued in "order of loan". Progress through the tallies was periodically announced in the *Gazette*. These tallies were interest-bearing and negotiable and in the absence of a banking system, paper money or a stock market, and at a time when a medieval repugnance to lending money for interest still lingered, investment in Exchequer debts was widespread.†

The paragraphs from the Exchequer were usually set in italic without heading at the end of the news in the third or fourth column. Notices of taxes and licences were also inserted as they fell due, and since many of the Exchequer debts were discharged on the revenue from specific imposts these notices were vital news to investors. Thus the *Gazette* contained financial news presented indirectly in official advertising.

Advertisements for lost property began to trickle into the *Gazette*. King and Court regularly mislaid their spotted, low-hung or liver-coloured dogs and an appeal for restoration was conveniently given publicity in the official paper. The *Gazette* was also the medium for those who suffered from the country-wide

*Quoted from All Souls College MS. 204 f. 81 by F. M. G. Evans, *The Principal Secretary of State* (Manchester 1923), p. 296.

†In 1672 by the "stop" of the Exchequer the Crown postponed repayment of principal although interest continued for some years.

depredations of horse thieves. Gradually the volume and variety of advertisements swelled. It was useful to the circulation that it should for even to modern readers this is a section of absorbing interest in old *Gazettes*. Home news could be obliquely culled from the insertions for those that offered rewards for information on thefts, murders and runaways briefly resumed facts, described persons and named places.

In 1674 Arlington anticipated impeachment by withdrawing from public life and Williamson earned the reward of being the best-informed man in the country when he was made Secretary for the Northern Department. The place cost him £5,000. He was unable long to enjoy it for in 1679, during the scare over the Popish plot, he was obliged to resign, his signature having in the course of his duties been set to commissions and warrants issued to recusants. Lord Sunderland, his successor, gave him the original price and compensation for the job.

During Williamson's period as Secretary he would have had less time to supervise Yard and in 1678 he appointed as gazetteer James Vernon, who during the 1670s had collected news for him in Holland. Vernon was—inevitably, to be chosen by Williamson—an Oxford man, the grandson of a London goldsmith and father of the future Admiral, "Grog" Vernon. He had diplomatic experience and before he joined Williamson had been secretary to the Duke of Monmouth. References to him as gazetteer* seem to have been the first public recognition of the post and probably mark the end of Williamson's immediate association with the journal he had created. Yard was to work in harness with Vernon for many years, sharing some posts, his lieutenant or successor in others.

Prerogative and Propaganda
Between 1679 and 1683 the licensing Act lapsed for Charles, fortified by subsidies from France, was able to prorogue and

*H.M.C., 11th Report, Appendix ii, 253; 12th Report, Appendix vii, 204.

dissolve Parliament as he wished. The *Gazette* might as a result have been exposed to competition. The lapse however coincided with the violent public feeling excited by Titus Oates' discovery of a "malignant plot" among Roman Catholics, and this was the mainstay of the periodicals that took advantage of the opportunity to appear.

The *Gazette* of May 3–6 1680 reported Chief Justice Scroggs' opinion on the prerogative: "That his Majesty may by law prohibit the printing and publishing of all newsbooks and pamphlets whatsoever, not licensed by his Majesty's authority, as manifestly tending to the breach of peace, and disturbance of the kingdom." This implicitly laid the authority for publishing the *Gazette* on the Crown. In practice action was not taken against unlicensed publications. The aftermath of the plot was a division between extreme Protestants and the moderate or Established Churchmen, and it was convenient to the government to permit opinion on both sides to be ventilated so long as such loyalists as L'Estrange were ready to beat down the most rabid Protestant propaganda in journals of their own.

The *Gazette* was unaffected by the passion on both sides for propaganda. This was the first occasion on which there was a challenge to the official paper of news as conceived by Williamson, that is, exempt from the Pepysian "folly" of editorial comment. To meet the needs of the King's government other short-lived journals of propaganda were allowed (but not authorized) to appear: the *Gazette* remained a journal of record.

Care to maintain the prestige of the *Gazette* brought reward. In 1683 the Turks besieged Vienna and the Austro-Turkish war created an abnormal demand for the official newspaper. English trade in the Mediterranean was already substantial, dominated by the Levant Company, and the effect of the war on the pockets and hopes of English shipowners and investors gave a big fillip to the sales of the *Gazette*. This was after the only surviving figures of the period, those for the Christmas quarter of 1679,

after Williamson had departed, when the total profits were
£95. 11s. and the revenue from advertisements £6 a week.*

In 1684 Charles II died and many of his ministers were
replaced by co-religionists of his Catholic brother James II.
Sunderland, Vernon and Yard were untouched, but at such times
of far-reaching change a journal like the *Gazette* was essential to
keep men informed. After the revival of the licensing Act
(1 Jac. II c. 17, sec. 15) there was no competition. Even so, no
other journal could have the authority of the *Gazette*, deriving
information from the source: the Court. It might not say all; but
what was said could be taken as correct.

*F. M. G. Evans, *The Principal Secretary of State* (Manchester 1923), p. 163.

Chapter III 1684—1702

Changing Contents of the Gazette

Charles during his last years and James during his whole reign
were positively defending the prerogative and this led to a shift in
the balance of the contents of the *Gazette*. At periods when action
had swiftly to be taken a government had always resorted to
proclamations, in general issued by the Council under the royal
seal. Although their force was ill-defined they were an accepted
exercise of the prerogative when time or other circumstances did
not permit the passing of a statute.*

A proclamation when printed had much in common with a
modern poster, being set out on a large sheet suitable for display
in public places. The *Gazette* offered a supplementary method of
making the substance of a proclamation quickly known and as the
issue of proclamations became frequent and their contents
significant their texts were increasingly reproduced. So the
Gazette became that described by Macaulay in the first volume of
his *History of England*: "The contents generally were a royal
proclamation, two or three Tory addresses, notices of two or
three promotions, an account of a skirmish between the imperial
troops and the Janissaries on the Danube, a description of a
highwayman, an announcement of a grand cockfight between
two persons of honour, and an advertisement offering a reward for
a strayed dog. . . . Whatever was communicated respecting
matters of the highest moment was communicated in the most
meagre and formal style."†

*The printing of proclamations belonged to the King's Printers' patent.
†Lord Macaulay: *History of England* (Albany edition 1908), i, 406.

25

Macaulay's contempt for news of Danubian battlefields was
not shared by contemporary readers of the *Gazette*, for the
statement that the circulation rose substantially during the
Austro-Turkish war came from an under-secretary who shared in
a moiety of the profits. English merchants knew their close
involvement with those distant lands where Europe and Asia
meet. Macaulay, Whig historian, disliked the prerogative
connection of the *Gazette* and he condemned it because it never
contained any intelligence "which it did not suit the purposes of
the Court to publish". That was true, and inevitable since the
Gazette was the journal of the Court; but much valuable news was
published and what did appear had the merit of accuracy so far as
this was possible to achieve.

The meagre and formal style was also inevitable. Neither Yard
nor Vernon was a professional journalist. They had the
experience usual in a civil servant of preparing memoranda and
composing official letters. The items they received were written
by correspondents of similar experience and the *Gazette* was
intended for readers with much the same qualifications. The real
matter for complaint was not the nature of the *Gazette* but the
lack of alternative newspapers for the general public.*

James Vernon

In March 1689 the young Lord Shrewsbury, who once declared
"I never read or write a letter",† became Secretary for the
Southern Department and Vernon as his secretary was kept fully
occupied. Shrewsbury was a favourite with William and Mary

---

*A striking instance of the meagre style occurred during the period when
William of Orange had been summoned to take over the throne in the last weeks of
1688 but James had not fled the country. The dismissed King returned to London in
mid-December and the *Gazette* without explanation printed an Order in Council
issued under his seal. The next issue reported William's arrival at St James's and his
reception by "all the nobility and other persons of the chiefest quality". James's final
departure was unnoticed. These issues gave a far from complete record: that was the
handicap of a journal of the Crown when the Crown was changing hands.

†See Shrewsbury's entry in *The Complete Peerage*.

for an outstanding charm of personality, but his relations with the King were clouded by suspicion of his Jacobite inclination. He resigned in 1690, whereupon Vernon transferred to his successor, returned to office in March 1694 and remained, first at the Northern Department and between 1695 and 1698 at the Southern, much of his time however being spent in self-imposed retirement in the country. During this period Vernon deputized as a Secretary of State and Yard became Shrewsbury's secretary. Vernon was sworn of the Privy Council in December 1697, and from 1698 until 1702 was continuously Secretary for one and sometimes both Departments. He and Yard were also successively Secretaries to the Lords Justices, in whose charge William left the country in his absences after Mary's death in 1694.

Although Vernon had little responsibility for decisions on foreign policy, which William retained in his own hands, he had a considerable administrative power not only within his own Department but through Shrewsbury with the Treasury and also with the Admiralty,* both of which were during this period in commission. In this respect Vernon was the forerunner of the senior civil servant, a careerist unsupported by claims of blood or fortune and without a primary political commitment.

Public Finance and the Gazette

The range of knowledge of public affairs possessed by Vernon, one-time Gazetteer himself and close colleague of Yard, was valuable to the *Gazette*, which, for instance, reported new developments in Treasury policy. The wars of the Grand Alliance against France brought benefit to this country's trade since it was freed from competition with the Dutch. To the Crown they were a drain that made it impossible for the King "to live of his own". The Treasury expanded in importance under a series

*G. F. James, "Some Further Aspects of Admiralty Administration 1689–1714" in *Bulletin of the Institute of Historical Research* (1939–40), xvii, 13, discusses the importance of the Secretaries of State in naval matters after the retirement of Pepys.

of able administrators, at the same time yielding to a measure of Parliamentary control.* Among the projects which revolutionized public finance was the founding in 1694 of the Bank of England. Hitherto there had been no public banking in this country and public credit, apart from the tally system, was regarded as impractical and undesirable. Shrewsbury took a leading part in the Bank's establishment, to the various stages of which the *Gazette* gave full publicity.

To hedge the risk the Million lottery was opened in the spring of 1694. Of the 100,000 £10 tickets the ordinary ones were to yield $6\frac{1}{2}$% for 16 years and 2,500 "fortunate numbers" a higher rate. The public had to be attracted, reassured and kept informed. Full particulars were printed in $1\frac{1}{2}$ columns of no. 2969 of the *Gazette*, April 23–26. The drafts of the commission for subscription to the Bank and the schedule of its charter received royal approval on July 7 and on the following day the Queen in Council ordered that the Treasury Commission "should prepare a notice for the *London Gazette* signifying the approval". This Order appears to be the first instance of a requirement to publish in the *Gazette*.

The details of the lottery and the Order in Council were printed as editorial matter and were set first as the main news of the day of issue. Later announcements, dates of court meetings, dividends and business news, were set as italic paragraphs at the end of the editorial matter, following the style of the official advertising of the Treasury and other public departments. They attracted more semi-official advertising from the East India Company, the Royal Africa and other merchant associations, which were henceforth regularly inserted in the *Gazette*.

*In 1690 a Commission was appointed by Parliament to examine the accounts of certain public departments, chiefly those connected with warfare. In no. 3009 of the *Gazette* the Admiralty Commissioners announced that because salaries would be paid to all secretaries, clerks and other officers, no fees or gratuities should be required or taken. Such steps were gradual: not until 1782 were Treasury clerks paid fixed salaries.

This accretion of City news came opportunely. In 1694 the Commons did not renew the licensing Act despite several bills. This lack of zeal for suppression had several causes. The Whigs, having secured in William a King committed to "govern according to the Statutes in Parliament agreed" were determined to keep the prerogative trammelled; those, chiefly Tories, who at least in Mary had been able to accept the unstained hereditary principle were weakened by her death in 1694. Publishers tested the new situation with magazines, such as the *Gentleman's Journal*, and then with thrice-weekly newspapers geared to the posts. For the first time since Muddiman's *Current Intelligence* the *Gazette* had competent and sustained competition.

The Rise of Professional Journalism

During the lapse of the licensing Act 1679–85 one of the most active publishers had been a Whig, Richard Baldwin, and on August 11 1694 he recommenced with a newspaper that after several changes of title emerged as the *Post Man* on October 22 1695. It was to be a formidable rival of the *Gazette* for the editor was a Huguenot journalist, Jean de Fonvive, regarded as "the glory and mirror of news writers ... as his news is good," a contemporary wrote, "so his style is excellent".* Against such a professional Yard had to compete. Although Lord Jersey once referred to "sprightly Yard's *Gazette*"† the evidence is that his style was not lively although he may have been a convivial colleague.

De Fonvive was however, like his employer, fervently anti-Catholic, anti-Bourbon and anti-Jacobite, and the *Post Man* was run to proclaim these antipathies. In November 1697 both were in custody for remarks "upon the Dauphin and the crooked disposition and body of his eldest son".‡ To find the grist of

*John Dunton, *Life and Errors* (1818), i, 428.

†Jersey to Prior, October 11 N.S. 1700, H.M.C., Bath MSS., iii, 421.

‡Leona Rostenberg, *Literary, Political, Scientific, Religious and Legal Publishing, Printing and Bookselling in England, 1551–1700* (New York 1965), ii, 391.

propaganda in the mishap of deformity does not belong to responsible journalism. Yet if the Press were to secure the freedom to appeal to public opinion there had to be a place for a vigorous, well-conducted journal such as the *Post Man*, for the most part accurate and its interest plainly announced. There also remained a place for the official journal presenting only fact and record.*

For members of the government and public service, justices of the peace and municipal officers, ambassadors and envoys, commercial agents and armed forces, the proclamations, promotions and Court news were essential and interesting. As our commerce and investment oversea expanded the *Gazette* was a link with the government at home, replacing except for confidential matters the official newsletters.† It retained its primacy for foreign news, and when the Holland mails did not arrive in time the fact was noted and their contents, which might include not only letters from the Hague but from Turin, Venice, Cologne, Paris and Brussels, were printed in an extraordinary or special issue when they contained news of particular importance.‡

As William kept foreign affairs in his own hands so he strenuously exerted what remained of prerogative power over the army. As his henchman he brought in William Blathwayt as Secretary at War, who transmitted to Yard the military matters requiring record in the *Gazette*. Like Vernon and the senior staff

---

*The *Gazette* was not always appreciated. In 1693 a newsletter reported that "on Thursday night was scattered about town a print of a sheet, entitled 'Observations on the *Gazette* in relation to the Turkey fleet, Battle of Landen, etc.' endeavouring to prove a partiality and inconsistency in these relations and to destroy the reputation of the public and *Gazette*." (C.S.P.D., 1693, September 2, p. 308).

†Thus an under-secretary writing abroad could reduce his correspondence by referring his colleague to the *Gazette*: "We have got past my Lord Jersey's entry which I leave to Mr Yard to embellish the *Gazette*" (Prior to Portland, January 10 N.S. 1699, H.M.C., Bath MSS., iii, 307), or "The Savoy Ambassador makes his entry to-day, as Mr Yard will tell more at large in the *Gazette* next Thursday" (Prior to Stanyan, January 8/19 1700, Bath MSS., iii, 394).

‡No. 2839, January 23–26 1692 had to be remade-up at the last moment because the mails came in "past eight at night". The first page is set in large type, the second in small. Extraordinaries were at this period not numbered.

at the Treasury, Blathwayt was a forerunner of the modern senior civil servant. Already the Palace at Whitehall was becoming the headquarters of a public service rather than a royal household. In 1698, after a fire destroyed much of the Cockpit on the north side of Whitehall, the rebuilt premises were allocated between the Secretaries of State and the Treasury, on a site partly occupied by the Treasury today. It was from here that for many years the *Gazette* was to be edited.

Chapter IV 1702–10

A Daily Newspaper

In the summer of 1702 Yard retired from the *Gazette*, having again followed in Vernon's steps by being appointed a Commissioner of Prizes at £500 a year. In May 1705 he died.* He was succeeded by Charles Delafaye, who had been employed in the department as a translator with particular responsibility for the *Gazette de Londres*.† An under-secretary had the task of looking through the *Gazette* before it went to the printer. The loss of Yard, who had been with the *Gazette* for over thirty years and who had worked in association with Vernon, left the *Gazette* editorially weakened when, a year after the opening of Anne's reign, the first English daily newspaper was founded.

No. 1 of the *Daily Courant* appeared on March 11 1703. It depended for its news on foreign journals from which it published paragraphs in translation. It was founded in the spring, the season when campaigning reopened, and soon established itself, supported by the growing prosperity of a trading nation and the excitement of the Continental wars which made Marlborough a name that resounded through Europe.

The growing power of the House of Commons and the absence of party organization obliged those who wished to mould political policy to depend on an appeal to influential opinion through the printed word. The minister who most skilfully

*Treasury Minute Book for 1702, p. 250; H.M.C., Buccleuch MSS., ii, 789.

†Delafaye had for some years a correspondence with the Abbé Rénaudot (of the *Gazette de Paris*), who was reputed to have a remarkable intelligence of English affairs (H.M.C., Bath MSS., iii, 269 and 282).

exploited printed propaganda was Robert Harley, who in May 1704 became Secretary for the Northern Department, his predecessor Sir Charles Hedges, an Admiralty lawyer, transferring to the Southern where he remained until 1706. Harley, like Godolphin, Anne's chief minister, had no addiction to party government, although he found his most useful allies among the Tories. Patient and imperturbable, a subtle politician to whom intrigue was a pleasure—he was nicknamed Robin the Trickster—his great talent lay in the manipulation of men. Handicapped by a bad delivery and a hesitancy of speech, Harley's natural medium was not oratory. His library, one of the most important collections now in the British Museum, testifies to his veneration of the written and printed word. A master of persuasion he sought to apply it through the Press.

Harleian Policy

In August 1702 he had suggested to Godolphin, then Lord Treasurer, that "It will be of great service to have some discreet writer of the Government's side if it were only to state facts right; for the generality err for want of knowledge, and being imposed upon by the stories raised by ill designing men".* His recognition of the importance of the "generality", the rise of political influence outside the cenacles of Whitehall and the Court, was not shared by Godolphin. Harley acted on his own account by engaging Daniel Defoe to write in his interest in the *Review* founded by the journalist in 1704; but for some years he ignored the *Gazette*. Delafaye was not, for reasons it was later alleged of economy, even appointed Gazetteer.

So far from supporting the *Gazette* Harley allowed it to be mocked by Defoe for failure "to state facts right". The official paper was lashed for minor mistakes, in sub-editing, such as a bishop being called Your Grace, and for downright inaccuracy, such as a report of the movements of our army on the Moselle

*Harley to Godolphin, B.M., Add. MSS., 28055, f. 3.

34

when we had no striking force near that river. The errors on military matters incensed Marlborough, and of one complaint which Godolphin passed on to Harley in 1705 the Lord Treasurer remarked that it was not the first "though much the sorest" about the *Gazette* from the General.* In the following year Marlborough demanded that reports from his own headquarters should be edited by Harley and sent to the *Post Man*, the *Gazette* being restricted to reports prepared by one of the staff of the War Office.†

De Fonvive of the Post Man

While Harley held his hand Hedges had irritatingly tried to mend matters by suggesting to the editor of the *Post Man*, still de Fonvive, that he should take over the *Gazette*. Unfortunately he made the proposal in terms quite unacceptable to a man who for years had had responsibility for a successful newspaper. What Hedges sought was "a clerk in his office to compile the *Gazette* and write now and then copies of letters". His powers of mind, slow to receive new ideas, failed to appreciate how the qualifications for journalism had changed since the lapse of the licensing Act. He looked back, perhaps, to Yard's first years in a corner of Arlington's office.

The successful thrice-weeklies, the *Post Man*, the *Postboy* and the *Flying Post*, and the single daily, the *Courant*, were not conducted by clerks able "now and then to copy letters". De Fonvive and his contemporaries were professionals accustomed to a responsibility that, though small compared with editors of later centuries, required initiative, discretion and experience as well as skill. Because the social status of the hack writers of the Press was immeasurably below the eminence of a Secretary of State—and was to remain so for the rest of the century—Hedges

*H.M.C., Bath MSS., i, 75. There is an excellent account of this period in the career of the *Gazette* in Laurence Hanson: *Government and the Press 1695–1763* (Oxford 1936).

†Marlborough to Harley, May 6 1706, H.M.C., Bath MSS., i, 81.

35

did not bother to consider the pride of an editor with a salary of £600 who paid his own clerk £50 a year.

It was to the more perceptive Harley that de Fonvive addressed his courteous letter of resentment at the offer. The writing of the *Gazette*, explained the journalist, "though judged trifling by such who never tried the difficulties thereof, requires more learning than some imagine, and a great deal of care to avoid blunders and contradictions; and as it must take up a man's whole time ought to have suitable encouragement". He condemned the way it had been left to a young clerk supervised by the under-secretaries "upon pretence of saving copy money". A realistic appointment, he contended, would have been that of a gentleman of parts who would make the *Gazette* his sole business at a salary of £500.*

During the following year, 1706, Hedges was superseded by Lord Sunderland, son-in-law to Marlborough, and Harley took notice of de Fonvive's advice to the extent of having Delafaye made full-time Gazetteer, still supervised by the two under-secretaries of each Department (one being Joseph Addison, another being Erasmus Lewis, Harley's confidant). At the same time the Secretaries were formally exhorted "to communicate such parts of their letters as they think fit to be published".†

The Gazetteer's Difficulties

The primitive method of compiling the *Gazette* from news in letters received by the Secretaries, with other items from private correspondents, had long since been expanded. The Treasury, the Privy Council, the Admiralty and the War Office were among the regular contributors, and inevitably the form in which messages were published did not always please those who provided the script. Besides the snub given when Marlborough withdrew his personal reports there had been Admiralty

*De Fonvive to Harley, July 18 1705, H.M.C., Portland MSS., viii, 187.

†H.M.C., Portland MSS., viii, 216.

complaints of Delafaye's presentation of naval material.* The Gazetteer had over-many masters. Yard had been protected by Williamson and Vernon, protected partly too, perhaps, by the relative immaturity of the public service. Delafaye was supervised by four under-secretaries, none powerful enough to intervene against generals and admirals. Not all the public departments welcomed publicity or believed that a *Gazette* should be published to give "information to the people". Others wanted to control the editing, unmindful of the difficulties created for the printer. The limited space of the single leaf made cutting and rewriting essential, but both offended departmental heads. These were handicaps of an official newspaper.

What Harley had in mind was a reconstruction of the *Gazette* which would turn it into a recognized department, if still a minor one, in the charge of a man acceptable to ministers and capable of editing without being called to account.

The Tonsons Print the Gazette
Since 1688 the *Gazette* had been printed by Edward Jones, an acting King's and Queen's Printer who took over Newcomb's house in the Savoy. Jones died in February 1706† and in the following year the printing was granted to Jacob Tonson, associated with his nephew also named Jacob. Thus the forty-year-old connection of the *Gazette* with the royal patentees was broken off.‡ The senior Tonson was well known as a bookseller and publisher and was also prominent politically as a member of the Whig Kit-Kat Club. Dryden, who found he drove a hard bargain, accused him of body odour:

*In 1704, when he implied that a battle had been avoided.

†For Jones see *The Life and Errors of John Dunton* edited by J. Nichols (1818) and Nichols, *Literary Anecdotes*, iv, 81. John Williams, manager of the royal printing house in Blackfriars and guardian of one of the patentees, applied to Harley for the vacancy without success (H.M.C., Portland MSS., viii, 384).

‡The first number printed by the Tonsons was that of March 1 1707. Their printing house was at the gate of Gray's Inn.

with leering look, bull faced and freckled fair . . .
and frowsy pores, that taint the ambient air.

Captain Steele becomes Gazetteer

Through the Kit-Kat Club Harley found a Gazetteer. It was
another member* who recommended to him a more impressive
figure than Delafaye: Richard Steele (later Sir), who after service
in the Guards had become a literary figure. To his credit in 1707
he had a few plays and what the diarist Hearne described as
"several romantic things". Tonson as his publisher knew him
well and had employed him as a reader. There was a more
personal connection between them as Steele had had a liaison with
Tonson's niece of which a child was born about 1700.†

Steele became Gazetteer on May 1 1707, Delafaye remaining
to assist him. He appears to have been instructed to study the
Gazette and other newspapers and to make recommendations "for
the advancement of the credit and income" of the official paper,
for during 1707 he prepared, probably for Sunderland, some
notes. His recommendations were four: that all embassies abroad
should supply a circular letter of news by every post; that the
Gazetteer's letters should travel by the "flying packet"; that he
should be able in the name of the Secretaries to prevent foreign
news packets from being delivered to other newspapers; and that
the *Gazette* should be published three times weekly on the post
days. Were he granted assistance on these lines he was "almost
confident" that he would be able to "raise the value of the paper
written by authority, and lessen the esteem of the rest among the
generality of the people".

Steele's proposals concentrated on the supply of foreign news.
They would ensure its rapid transmission and exclusiveness and
would free the *Gazette* of the handicap of a periodicity below

*Arthur Mainwaring, M.P.

†*The Correspondence of Richard Steele* edited by Rae Blanchard (Oxford 1941)
from which subsequent quotations from Steele's letters are taken.

38

contemporaries. The real problem was untouched. He made no claim for editorial independence, nor did he discuss the rights or scope of the Gazetteer.

In the first few days of office he ran into the trouble familiar to Delafaye when Prince George of Denmark, then Lord High Admiral, complained of a report which Steele contended he had been told by Sunderland's under-secretary to publish.* Explaining the situation to Sunderland he asked for his protection. Yet he did not quarrel with his dependence on the Secretary. He accepted that the Gazetteer could not be the "authority" for publication. He saw the post as the "lowest minister of State", where he worked "according to order".†

Concurrently with the Prince's complaint the Admiralty had also advised Steele not to publish a certain report until they had prepared it for him. He consulted Addison, one of Sunderland's under-secretaries, who suggested that further delay would imply that "the Government had a mind to stifle the account". Steele therefore went to the Admiralty and made his own report from their documents. In this instance Steele, regarding the Secretary as representing "authority", had overridden the Admiralty.

Steele's Friends

In addition to Addison at Steele's elbow there was Jonathan Swift, who was constantly visiting them at the Cockpit. In 1708 Swift was a new-found friend who rapidly gained sufficient influence to persuade Steele to make editorial changes. In August 1708 Swift wrote to an Irish correspondent that "in the last *Gazette* it was certainly affirmed that there would be a battle; but the copy coming to the office to be corrected I prevailed with them to let me soften the phrase a little, so as to leave some room for possibilities".‡ A trio of greater distinction than Addison, Steele

*Steele to Sunderland, May 10 1707 *Correspondence*, p. 21.
†*Mr Steele's Apology for Himself and his Writings* (1714) p. 81.
‡Swift to Archbishop King, August 28 1708, *The Correspondence of Jonathan Swift*, edited by F. Elrington Ball (1910), p. 107.

and Swift can hardly be imagined: yet Steele was later to remark on "the reproaches he heard every Gazette day against the writer of it".* From whom came these reproaches? The "generality"? Or colleagues in the public service, complaining as Arlington's office had complained of Yard?

Steele's efforts together with thrice-weekly publication, which was adopted in June 1709 with no. 4552, did not succeed in persuading the "generality" to prefer the *Gazette*. The circulation, calculated to be about 6,000 in 1704,† was in June 1710 on average 5,400 copies sold to the general public with a further 1,087 distributed free to government officials, post-masters and embassies at home and abroad. Sunderland received a moiety of £24. 3s. 8d. on six issues out of which varying sums were paid to eight people in his Department.‡ As the moiety had increased since 1679, so had the advertisement revenue: £18 in one week, £20. 10s. in a second.

The job was scarcely suited to a writer of Steele's talent for he was bound, so he revealed,* by "the rule observed by all ministries [i.e. of whatever political colour], to keep that paper very innocent and very insipid". This was the formal style abhorrent to Macaulay. Steele offset its effect on him by embarking upon his own newspaper, the *Tatler*, a bi-weekly begun in April 1709§ which he hoped to run in tandem with the *Gazette*. Sometimes he used the same items rephrased to suit a different readership, sometimes he selected items appropriate for the one or the other.

Apology (1714), p. 81.

†J. R. Sutherland, "The Circulation of Newspapers and Literary Periodicals 1700–1730", in *The Library*, 4th series (1934–35), xv, 110.

‡P.R.O., S.P. 34, piece 12, f. 89 is an account for the "English Gazette" June 1–3 1710. Steele was separately paid £11. 12s. and Delafaye £2. 0s. 2d. Some 2,000 copies were left on the printer's hands every post day. It is possible that he used some of them for his own advantage.

§No. 1 appeared on April 12. See *Studies in the early English periodicals* (Chapel Hill 1958) edited by Richmond P. Bond for a discussion of Steele's conduct of the two papers.

Steele Dismissed

His freedom of editorial control of the *Tatler* was his downfall as
Gazetteer. During 1710 divided opinions on the continuance of
war with France were vigorously aired in the Press. Harley was
supported by the extremely successful *Examiner*, begun on
August 3 1710, with which Swift became associated. Steele
impulsively showed his political hand in the *Tatler*, attacking
Harley in a satire supposedly written by a stage prompter, which
ridiculed the ministry by treating changes in it as changes of
theatrical management. On September 10 1710 Swift told Stella
that "Steele will certainly lose his Gazetteer's place, all the world
detesting his engaging in the parties". All the world was an
ample term: it was the *Examiner* that accused Steele of having
"violated the most solemn repeated promises, and that perfect
neutrality which he had engaged to maintain".

That Steele's offence had been in the *Tatler*, not the *Gazette*,
did not save him. The general election which took place that
autumn was fought hard by Harley and his friends and the Tories,
and the *Gazette* was a valuable adjunct. Harley was told that the
Whigs in the North Riding of Yorkshire "(according to their old
laudable custom everywhere) are perpetually trumping up some
lying story or other to blacken their opponents; but Paul
Joddrell's attestation in a late *Gazette* has so opened the eyes of
abundance of misled people, even of the meanest, that truth itself
coming from that party would hardly be believed".*

So Steele's Gazetteership, which had opened with such
promise for "the advancement of the credit and income" of the
official paper, floundered in political cross currents. Never again
was so gifted an editor to be appointed, never again was there a
serious prospect that for early and inclusive news the *Gazette*
would in circulation outstrip all contemporaries and be a genuine
newspaper buttressed by the authority of the Crown. Harley,
immeasurably less single-minded and ambitious than Williamson,

*J. Durden to Harley, October 13 1710, H.M.C., Portland MSS., iv, 613.

would not cut through the bonds that the increasing number and power of government officials laid upon the *Gazette* in the name of "authority". Admiralty and War Office, Privy Council and Treasury, and others claimed the right to authorize: what a Gazetteer needed was an overriding authority, whether in himself or in a single minister. He needed also to be uncommitted to party doctrines.

Harley's methods were devious, his assumption of command cautious, and ministerially he faltered. At the crucial time of the *Gazette*'s development, when it, like the public service, was in a state of flux and growth, Harley was not by temperament the strong minister Steele needed. His achievement was that he kept comment out of the *Gazette* at a time when violent party argument was the stuff of journalism. It was not "perfect" in neutrality, but in the eighteenth century the Crown was not perfect in neutrality. Without Harley's effort for a journal of fact and record the *Gazette* might not have survived, but the price was high, for the official newspaper of the Crown was the most "insipid" of all newspapers.

Chapter V 1710–27

Swift and the Gazette

After Tory success in the 1710 election Harley (later
Lord Oxford) became Lord Treasurer, and Henry St John (later
Lord Bolingbroke) Secretary for the Northern Department
1710–13 and for the Southern 1713–14. One of the finest orators
of the century—a century that included Chatham—St John was
also a distinguished writer. His mind ranged further and faster
than Harley's, his character was pressing and active; and his
talent was for propaganda. While he and Swift continually
discussed the management of the Press and the preparation of
of articles and pamphlets, they left the *Gazette* to clerks. They
disregarded applications from Abel Boyer and Abel Roper, two
outstanding contemporary editors, because they had, or had had
Whig sympathies.* Swift, who had been sick of the same fever,
detested them.

The Irishman did not however neglect the *Gazette* as a source
of profit to friends for in the summer of 1711 he engineered the
transfer of the printing from the Tonsons to his own publisher,
Benjamin Tooke, and his associate John Barber of Lambeth Hill,
printer to the City of London. By July 29 Swift was claiming to
Stella that he had "got the *Gazette*" for Tooke and that it would
be worth £300. Steele protested that there was good reason to

*Boyer was like de Fonvive a Huguenot who had been connected with journalism
since the beginning of the reign. He wrote to Harley on October 17 1710
(H.M.C., Portland MSS., iv, 615). Solicitations on behalf of Roper were addressed
to Lord Dartmouth, Secretary of State, on June 26 and September 28 1710
(H.M.C., Dartmouth MSS., v, 296).

change the writer of the journal to one agreeable to the ministry, but "that reason methinks, cannot bear against the printer of it, who is mechanically to do as he is ordered". The Tonsons however, being noted Whigs, could hardly expect to retain the printing under an aggressively Tory ministry and, the *Examiner* being at this time discontinued, Barber as its printer was free to house another periodical.*

Swift was jubilant at his success, which earned him some fine City dinners, and in September he also "got" for Barber the printing of the South Sea Company, the Tory answer to the Bank of England. At this period Tooke and Barber also obtained a 30-year lease of the Queen's Printers' patent which they later sold at a profit. The Gazetteership was another plum which Swift secured for a protégé, William King, a doctor of law and as unlikely a *Gazette* writer as Steele, his literary reputation resting on humorous dialogues.

The Editorial Burden

Amiable, easy-going and indigent, King had gained experience of journalism in the best contemporary school as one of the editors of the *Examiner*. In the past he had held several official posts he had treated as sinecures, but misfortune had affected his health and pocket. Swift had to guarantee the diligence and sobriety of the "poor, starving wit", who was granted a salary of £200 a year.†

Steele had found the thrice-weekly publication of the *Gazette* a burden. His correspondence with his wife is sprinkled with affectionate notes written at "One in the morning. From the Press", or "Near ten at night. Secretary's office", to explain the failure to be home at an expected hour because, for instance, "there are new orders come hither from the Secretary's which

*Swift wrote to Stella on July 26 that the change of printer was none of his doing but changed his tune on the 29th. Steele to James Brydges, July 25, *Correspondence*, p. 48.

†Swift to Stella on December 19 and 31 1711.

GAZETTE DE LONDRES.

Publiée avec Privilége.

Depuis le Jeudi 12, jusqu'au Lundi 16 Août 1669. V. S.

De Lyme, le 11 Août 1669.

LE 9 de ce mois, 2 Bâtimans de ce Pôrt, qu'on nomme le Lis Rôse, & le François, arrivérent ici, chargez de toiles de Morlaix, où ils ont laissé plusieurs Personnes de qualité assemblées pour aviser aus meilleurs moïens de lever quantité de Matelots, & de Charpentiers, & les envoïer a Brest, où l'on équipe plusieurs Navires, destinez pour la Méditerranée.

De Déle, le 12 Août 1669.

Un Navire est, depuis peu, arrivé ici, du Détroit, d'où en revenant il a été rançontré par plusieurs Vaisseaux de guerre d'Alger, qui lui ont laissé continuër sa route sans aucun empêchemant.

De Moscou, le 14 Juillet 1669.

L'on a, depuis peu, tenu plusieurs Conférances en cête Cour, touchant l'établissemant du Commerce avec les Princes Etrangers, ausquelles on a mandé les Facteurs du Grand Duc pour y donner leurs Avis : mais l'on n'y a, encore, rien conclu. Nous attandons, avec impatiance, l'affermissemant d'une bonne intelligence entre cête Couronne, & celle de Pologne : & depuis qu'il court un Bruit que les Tazares minutent quêque Expédition il y a un grand Capitaine, nommé Casas Gregori Romadanski, qui a ordre de prandre sa marche vers les Fronsières de Tartarie avec un puissant Corps d'Armée pour les obsérver. Le Sieur Pierre Vasilewich Charemetoff, Prémier Ministre d'Etat, &, ci-devant, Gouverneur de Kiovie a été nommé pour aller en qualité d'Ambassadeur Extraordinaire en Pologne, complimenter le Roi sur son heureus avènemant à la Couronne.

De Tanger, le 15 Juillet 1669.

Les Mores, nos Ennemis ont, depuis peu, paru en nômbre considérable, tant de Cavalérie, que d'Infanterie autour de nos Lignes, & tâché par des Embuscades d'attirer nos gens dans le danger : mais nos canons & nôtre mousquéterie les ont obligez à se retirer avec quêque perte. La derniére Entreprise de cête nature qu'ils ont faite ce fut le 2 de ce mois : mais il y a apparance que leur mauvais succès les a découragez d'en faire plus de semblables : du moins, l'on n'en a pas vû paroistre beaucoup depuis ce jour-là. L'Empereur de Maroc a, depuis peu, réduit à son Obéissance quantité de Rebelles, qui faisoient leur demeure sur le haut des montagnes. Ceus de Salé ont 5, ou 6 Navires de guerre en Mer, avec lesquels ils ont, naguéres, fait des Prises considérables : mais l'on espére qu'ils seront, bien-tôt, mis à la raison, & que le Commerce de ces Mers sera déliuré de leurs Courses.

De Warsovie, le 2 Août 1669. N. S.

Il y a environ 8 jours que nous reçeûmes des Lettres de l'Ukraine, qui portoient que les Tartares étoit à la tête d'une Armée de 40 mille hommes, avec lesquels si avoit joint les Cosaques en dessein de faire Irruption dans la Pologne. Quoi que nous eussions reçu de bonne main ces Nouvelles nous avions, néanmoins, de la peine à les croître, jusqu'à ce qu'elles nous eussent été confirmées par Lettres de Leopolis en Russie, datées du 26 Juillet, qui ajoûtent que les Habitans du plat-Païs des Fronsières en avoient déia pris l'alarme, & s'étoient retirez dans Leopolis, & autres Places fortes, avec leur Bétail, & le meilleur de leurs Meubles : & que l'Armée de la Couronne a tant avis qu'ils étoient en si grand nombre qu'elle n'étoit pas assez forte pour leur faire tête en campagne, elle avoit abandonné ses anciens Quartiers, & s'étoit aussi, retirée dans Leopolis. Cependant, les Turcs ne manquent pas de prandre leurs avantages contre nous : le Visir aiant prêté Sermant d'exécuter le Traité fait avec les Cosaques Rebelles, qui contient les Articles, qui ensuivent. 1. Qu'il n'abolira point leur Religion, qui est conforme à l'Eglise Grecque, & ne souffrira point que l'on bâtisse aucunes Mosquées dans l'Ukraine. 2. Que leur Clergé, & autres Personnes seront maintenus en une pleine, & entiére liberté, & en tous les Priviléges, Franchises, & Immunitez dont ils ont, ci-devant, ioüi, avec exemption de toutes Contributions, & Subsides. 3. Qu'il ne souffrira point que l'on abbatte, ou démolisse aucunes Eglises Russiennes. 4. Que les Affaires seront réglées de telle sorte que les Cosaques seront Maîtres absolus de la moitié du Duché de Russie, qui est contrigüe aus Territoires de Jaroslavie, tout ainsi que leurs Ancêtres en ont ioüi, quoi que, néanmoins, usurpée quant à présent, par les Polonois. Que les Cosaques seront déchargez du paiemant de la somme de 12 mille Florins, qu'ils éroient obligez de paier à la Pologne : & que si l'on en demande quêqu'une à l'avenir, elle sera paiée par la Cour Ottomane à leur acquit. 6. Que les Cosaques choisiront pour leur Général telle Personne que bon leur semblera. 7, & finalemant, que pour plus grande seureté il y aura un Parti considérable de Turcs, & de Tartares posté sur les Fronsières. Les calamitez éminantes dont nous sommes menacez ont fait prandre résolution au Roi, de l'avis de son Conseil, de dépêcher un Courier à l'Archêvêque de Gneisne, qui demeure environ à 15 Lieuës de cête ville, par lequel Sa Majesté lui mande d'y venir en diligence pour expédier ses Lettres Circulaires addressantes à la Noblesse avec ordre de se mettre sous les armes pour la deffaite du Roïaume, le Roi n'en aïant pas le Pouvoir, à ce qu'il semble, jusqu'à ce qu'il soit couronné. L'on apprêhende d'autant plus les sinistres événemans de cête Invasion, que l'Arriereban de la Noblesse ne l'oblige qu'à servir 15 jours durant à ses dépens, après lequel tems passé elle doit recevoir sa Paie ainsi que l'Armée : & que l'on n'a, encore, avisé à aucuns moïens de lever de l'Argent ; le Conseil des Sénateurs ne pouvant être, si tôt, assemblé, d'autant qu'ils se font tous retirez en leurs Maisons de campagne : ce n'est pas que tous les Polonois ne paroissent remplis de courage, & que l'on répute pour bon Augure du succès, qui leur doit arriver. Un Courier de Paris, arrivé ici, de Paris, qui a apporté ordre à l'Evêque de Besiers, Ambassadeur de France, de s'y en retourner promptemant : c'est pourquoi il doit prandre ce soir, son Audiance de congé du Roi. Pour l'Ambassadeur de Sa Majesté Impériale il a reçu ordre de demeurer encore ici quêques jours : mais il prandra si bien ses mesures pour s'en retourner à Vienne, qu'il sera en sorte d'être de retour en cête ville dans le 29 Septembre, pour la Cérémonie du Couronnemant du Roi, qui se doit faire à Cracovie.

De Cologne, le 16 Août 1669. N. S.

Les Avis d'Aremberg contiennent que l'Evêque de Strasbourg s'en va à Hildesheim, d'où il est Grand Prévost, pour s'en retourner, après, en son Evêché. L'Evêque de Munster n'est pas, encore, résolu de consantir à l'élargissemant du Sieur Erytagh, qui est Suiet de la Princesse de la Frise Orientale. Ce Prélat a passé beaucoup de tems à Coesuelt, Boikelo, & à Staremberg sur les Fronsières de son Païs.

De Paris, le 20 Août 1669. N. S.

Le Roi aiant appris la mort du Duc de Beaufor, a donné au Comte de Vermandois, son Fils Naturel, sa Charge d'Amiral

---

Gazette de Londres A version of the *Gazette* was prepared in French for circulation abroad.
Reproduced by courtesy of the British Museum

The Oxford Gazette.

Published by Authority.

Oxon. Nov. 7.

THis day the Reverend Dr. *Walter Blandford*, Warden of *Wadham Colledge* in this University, was Elected Lord Bishop of this See, vacant by the death of Dr. *Paul*, late Bishop here.

Oxon. Nov. 12. This day His Majesty in Council, according to the usual custom, having the Roll of Sheriffs presented to him, pricked these persons following to be Sheriffs for the succeeding Year, in their respective Counties of *England* and *Wales*.

Berks.	Basil Brent, *Esquire.*
Bedford.	Tho: Snagge, *Esq;*
Buckingham.	Simon Bennet, *Esq;*
Cumberland.	Sir William Dalston, *Baronet.*
Chester.	Sir John Arderne, *Knight.*
Cambridge.	Sir Tho: Willis, *Kt. and Baronet.*
Cornwal.	Tho: Dorrel, *Esq;*
Devon.	John Kelland, *Esq;*
Dorset.	Roger Clavel, *Esq;*
Derby.	Sir Samuel Sleigh, *Knight.*
Yorkshire.	Sir Francis Cobb, *Knight.*
Essex.	Sir Heneage Fetherston, *Baronet.*
Gloucester.	Sir Richard Cox, *Baronet.*
Hertford.	Sir Jonathan Keat, *Baronet.*
Hereford.	Tho: Rod, *Esq;*
Kent.	Sir Humphrey Miller, *Baronet.*
Lancaster.	William Spencer, *Esq;*
Leicester.	Sir Edward Smith, *Baronet.*
Lincoln.	Sir John Brownlow, *Kt. and Baronet.*
Monmouth.	Walter Morgan of Landillo Patholly, *Esq;*
Northumberland.	Will.m Middleton, *Esq;*
Northampton.	Joseph Hanbury, *Esq;*
Norfolk.	Sir John Hobard, *Baronet.*
Nottingham.	John White of Corgrave, *Esq;*
Oxford.	Tho: Wheate *of* Glymston, *Esq;*
Rutland.	Charles Halford, *Esq;*
Shropshire.	Sir Humph: Briggs.
Somerset.	Sir Hugh Smith, *Baronet.*
Stafford.	Fran: Leveson, *alias* Fowler, *Esq;*
Suffolk.	Sir Edmond Bacon, *Baronet.*
Southampton.	Tho: Neale, *Esq;*
Surrey.	Sir John Evelyn, *Baronet.*
Sussex.	Robert Fowle, *Esq;*
Warwick.	Charles Bentley, *Esq;*
Worcester.	Sir William Cooks of Norgrave, *Kt.*
Wilts.	Sir John Weld, *Knight.*
Anglesey.	Rowland Bulkley, *Esq;*
Brecknock.	Hugh Powel, *Esq;*
Cardigan.	James Stedman, *Esq;*
Carnarvon.	Tho: Maderne, *Esq.*
Denbigh.	Sir Charles Goodman.
Flint.	Sir Roger Mostyn.
Glamorgan.	William Basset of Brabeskin, *Esq;*
Merioneth.	Lewis Lloyd, *Esq;*
Montgomry.	Ed: Kynaston, *Esq;*
Pembroke.	Sir Herbert Perrot.
Radnor.	Nich: Taylor, *Esq;*
Carmarthen.	William Lloyd, *Esq;*

Paris, Nov. 14. Monsieur *de Turenne* is not yet returned, but expected here every day. Most of the Gentry of *Niverness* & *Auxerge* are said to have withdrawn themselves, and got into a place of strength, one Monsieur *de Canillac* having been put to death by the Commissioners of the *Grands Iours*: It seems they had laid some new Taxes or Impositions on those parts: There are Troups marching against them, and it is thought they will soon be reduced. My Lord *Aubigny* Lord *Almonry* to her Majesty, having layen sick some time here of an Hydropsie attended with a Flux, is this week dead.

Paris November. 18. The *Mareschal de Turenne* arrived here on Sunday last from the Frontiers, whence he brings account that the Succors intended against the Prince of *Munster* had passed in small parties, and that they had been received at *Maestriche* by *Monsieur Bevering* in the name of the States General.

Guernzy, Octob. 30. Yesterday came into our Road the *Unity* Frigot, Captain *Trafford* Commander, who brought in a Prize Captain *John Giffen* of *Flushing*, being a Privateer of 7 Guns, and 45. Men.

Chattham Nov. 4. Captain *Eliot* Commander of the *Saphire* has taken 3 Busses, two of them out of 50 at the *Dogger-sands*, under the Protection of four of their Men of War. In his passage home, 'tis said, he saw several tops of Ships, Masts, &c. which seemed to be the effects of some Wrecks which God be thanked we do not hear to have been any of the *English* Ships.

Oxon. Nov. 12. Not knowing what accompt the Publick has hitherto received of the Progress of the Prince of *Munster*'s Armes we have thought it not improper without further repetiton, to give an account of such places as he at present stands possest of in the Enemies Countrey *viz.* The Castle and Territory of *Boreta*, (being of right his own, and for many years unjustly detained from him) the Castle of *Litchtouve de* and the Towns of *Lechten*, *Datcchem*, *Direpenheim*, *Gaer*, *Enschede*, *Oldenstl*, *Octhmenschen*, *Hardenburg*, *Ommea*, *Venwildenberg*, *Keppel*, *Almeloe*, *Hengel*, *Gramsberg*, and *Venenebrag*, and now more lately *Winschol*, with the Fort of *Bruggen scanz*, the Castle of *Wedde*, and the Cloyster of *Appel*, out of which a party of his had some time before been forced by the *Hollanders*. And it is confirmed to us by several good hands from *Brussels*, that he has taken the strong Fort of *Boutaine*, and *Reid*, a Sea-port scituate near *Dramme* and *Delpfs* ist', in diverse of which places His Highness has left very considerable Garrisons, besides his Field-Army, which consists of 18000 Foot, and 6000 Horse effective.

Deale, Nov. 8. The wind, since my last continues very high, but I hear of no harm done yet. The *Phœnix* hath brought in a Prize here.

Norwich, Nov. 8. I lately received from a good hand in *Rochel* dated *Oct.* 28. a short account of the taking the Island St. *Ustache*, which for the manner of the attempt, may not be unworthy the communication ; it was brought by a *French West-India* ship which came from St. *Christophers* about 3 leagues from it, and runs thus, That on the 12 of *Aug.* about 300 of the Forces belonging to *Jamaica* went thither with a resolution of an attaque. There is but one landing place in the whole Island, and that of such difficult access, that but 2 at most can go abreast, up an ascent to an eminent place, in the top of which was a strong Fort, which on this occasion had been well furnished with powder & Guns left by *De Ruyter*, and man'd with 450 soldiers, who were nevertheless so surprised at the boldness of the Undertaking, that they delivered themselves up with very little resistance.

Plymouth, Nov. 5. The Weather of late hath been very

A

very tempestuous on these Coasts, and we hear that a Dutch man or Hamburger (uncertain yet whether) hath been cast away at the Barre. A ship from Virginia belonging to London was cast away about 3 Leagues from this place, and 5 men lost; and another Virginia ship driven ashore but got off without much damage.

Chester, Nov. 11. This City and Country, (thanks be to God) remain in good health, without the least Infection. We have advice from Duncannon in Ireland, That the Governor, Sir Nicholas Aymorer hath secured a Ship bound from Guinne, worth in Gold dust, and other rich Commodities, 50000 l. which by storm was forced into that River. The Particulars what she is, whither bound, and upon whose account is not yet said. The Winds have been so cross here, that five Irish Pacquets are said to be still detained at Holy-Head, where of late there fell a storm of Hail so great, that some affirm, several grains were taken up, which were four inches, about.

Southwould, Nov. 13. Yesternight came by this Town a Fleet of loden Colliers, about 30 Sail of great Ships, and many small Vessels were in sight before night: what passed afterward we know not; 'tis hoped this night or to morrow morning they will be in the River of Thames.

Falmouth, Nov. 8. A small Vessel of Apsom was cast away on this Coast, loaden with Oranges and Lemmons, but the men were saved.

Hull, Nov. 10. This day arrived several Ships from New-Castle and Scarborough, which assure us that Coast is all clear. This day sailed his Majesties Ship the Bull, and in her Convoy three Ships for Yarmouth Peer, as also the Victualling Ships and Hoy laden with Timber for the use of the Navy.

Dublin, Nov. 4. The House of Commons expressing their sad resentment that some Persons who had the Honor of being Members of that House, and consequently were admitted to consult of the weighty affaires of the Kingdom, should be so far debaucht from their duty, as Traitorously to conspire against the Government, and joyn themselves in raising a Rebellion particularly designed on the 21 of May, 1663. did on the 2d instant (the first time of their meeting by reason of the several necessary Prorogations) by Declaration testifie their just Detestation and Abhorrence of that Traiterous Engagement, & that though many other weighty Affairs were at present before them, they would in the first place enter upon the consideration of that particular, returning their most humble and hearty thanks to his Grace the Lord Lieutenant, whose singular prudence and circumspection had prevented its progress, and assuring him of their constant Loyalty to his Majesty, and their obedience to him as their Governour; This declaration was presented to the Lord Lieutenant by their Speaker, and in consequence of it, they past this Vote:

Nov. 4th. 1664. Whereas several Members of this House (viz.) Robert Shapcote, John Chambers, Thomas Boyd, Alexander Staples, Abel Warren, John Ruxton, and Thomas Sea Esquires had been by Vote of this House suspended from sitting in the House until the farther pleasure of the House be known; and to the end it may be accordingly signified; Ordered upon the Question, that this House do appoint Thursday morning next at 10 of the clock to hear and every the said Persons that have any defence to make for themselves against the Charge of Treason whereof they are accused, otherwise this House will then proceed to give judgment upon the Evidence now before them.

Oxon. Nov. 13. This Morning arrived here from Tangier, Major Palmes Fairbone, Major of Colonel Norwoods Regiment in that Garrison, who parted from thence the 16th past, and arrived at Calais in 15 days where he was kept by the violent cross Weather nine days for a Passage. By him we have a particular account of the

prosperous condition of that place, and of the great care and industry of the Lord Bellosis, his Majestic Governor there, in providing this important place with all necessaries that may render it in this conjuncture as well secure to it self, as of protection and defence to the shipping of this Nation, in their passage to and from the Straight, of which the following Relation brought by the same hand gives us an eminent instance: Upon the 13th past, it happened that certain Victuallers, intended for Tangier, under the Convoy of the Merlin Frigot of 12 guns, Captain Haward Commander (the same that some months since, in a small West-country Vessel, with 8 men and a boy, so bravely master'd the Turks man of War, to whom several Merchants ships, to the number of 16, or 17, had joined themselves, parting with the Fox Frigot, and a Merchant-man, bound for Sally, on a particular design, & at the expence of a private Merchant-off of Cape Sparta, the Merchant-men (as their custom is) saluting those 2 at their going off for Sally, gave notice to 5 Dutch men of War already under Sail before the Bay of Cadiz, the Admiral of 56 Guns, one of 45, one of 40, and two of 36 each, who having the wind at N.W. were presently up with ours. The Merlin was the headmost, & perceived not the Dutch, who came in the stern (it seems) till they had possessed themselves of two Victuallers, and one Merchant-man bound for Legorn, Capt. Allen Commander. He immediately tacked about, & so mawled them for 4 hours, that our whole Fleet had time to escape into the Bay of Tangier, Having received several shots under water, his masts & tackling much mauled; and perceiving the headmost of the Dutch Ships, the Charles a ship of 45 guns, who had done him the most mischief, to be making after our Fleet, and that she would inevitably take them all, he frankly run himself aboard her, where he fought a full hour board and board: Till at length the Captain being shot through the shoulder with the Musket bullet, and grazed cross the fore-head with another, having now seen all his Men, save 8 fall dead, or desperately wounded by his side; he was at last brought to yield, and was carried into Cadiz, where he is said to be in a hopeful way of recovery.

The Dutch are said to have pursued our Merchants up to the very mould of Tangier, whence, by the fire of the great battery & of the Musketeers the Lord Bellosis had very seasonably disposed there, they were beat off & the Fleet of Merchants preserved, riding in defiance of them. The Tunis Merchants a Ship of 28 Guns, behaved her self very well in this occasion, and so galled the Dutch at the former part of the action, that they confess they were upon the point once of quitting the Merlin.

Oxon. Nov. 14. The Flanders and Holland Maies having miss'd us for several Posts together by reason of the cross winds as is supposed, we have no late News from those parts: Only it is assured by the Letters from Paris 8 instant, that General Gorgas has certainly gained a passage upon the Hollanders, whereby he has forced those 5000 of the Prince of Munster's men, which were said to be shut up near Winshotten by Prince Maurice's Troops, having kill'd the greatest part of those that were set to maintain the Post, and taken five piece of Cannon. These letters say farther, that the States of the Province of Holland were so nettled at the printing the Proposition of the Province of Overysel concerning the re establishment of the Prince of Orange, that they ordered it forthwith to be supprest, and fell upon debate whether a Proclamation should not be issued for prohibiting the like addresses for the future, but it found such opposition even from Amsterdam it self, that they were forced to lay it aside. General Wrangel is said to have arriv'd 15 past old stile in Pomer-land, attended with 3 men of War, and three other Vessels laden with ammunition.

The account of the weekly Bill at London, runs thus; Total, 1359. Plague, 1050. Dec eased 418.

Oxon, Printed by Leonard Litchfield, and Re-printed at London, for the use of some Merchants and Gentlemen, who desired them.

The London Gazette.

Numb. 2984.

Publiſhed by Authority.

From **Thurſday** June 7. to **Monday** June 11. 1694.

At the Court at *White-Hall,*
the 7th of *June,* 1694.

PRESENT,

Lord Archbiſhop of *Canter-bury.*	Earl of *Montagu.*
Lord Keeper.	Earl of *Ranelagh.*
Lord Privy Seal.	Viſcount *Dxrſley.*
Duke of *Shrewsbury.*	Lord *Cornwallis.*
Duke of *Bedford.*	Lord *Godolphin.*
Duke of *Devonſhire.*	Mr. Secretary *Trenchard.*
Marquis of *Winchelter.*	Mr. Chancellor of the Ex-chequer.
Earl of *Oxford.*	Maſter of the Rolls.
Earl of *Bridgwater.*	Sir *Henry Goodricke.*
Earl of *Stamford.*	

THE annexed Draft of a Commiſſion, for taking Subſcriptions for the Bank of England, together with a Schedule containing the Draft of the Charter, mentioned in the ſaid Commiſſion to which it is annexed, and whereunto the ſame hath Reference, being Read and Approved at this Board. It is Ordered by Her Majeſty in Council, That the Right Honorable the Lords Commiſſioners of the Treaſury, do preſent the ſame to Her Majeſty for Her Royal Signature, in order to paſs the Great Seal of England.

John Nicholas.

At the Court at *White-Hall,*
the 8th of *June,* 1694.

PRESENT,

The Queens moſt Excellent Majeſty in Council.

IT is this day Ordered by Her Majeſty in Council, That the Right Honorable the Lords Commiſſioners of the Treaſury, do prepare an Advertiſement to be inſerted in next Mondays Gazette, to give Notice, That the Commiſſion and Draft of a Charter, for the Corporation of the Bank of England, is Approved, and Signed by Her Majeſty, in order to paſs the Great Seal of England.

John Nicholas.

In purſuance of the foregoing Order, Theſe are to give Notice, That the Warrant for the ſaid Commiſſion, Signed by Her Majeſty, will forthwith be paſſed under the Great Seal of England, with a Schedule thereunto annext, containing the ſubſtance of the Charter which is to Paſs in like manner, immediately after the firſt day of Auguſt next, if the Sum of Twelve hundred Thouſand Pounds, or one Moiety, or more, thereof, ſhall be Subſcribed by that time, or ſooner if the whole Twelve hundred Thouſand Pounds ſhall be ſooner Subſcribed. And that Their Majeſties Commiſſioners will, within very few days, meet at Mercers-Chappel in Cheapſide, London, to receive as well the ſaid Subſcriptions, as the firſt Fourth part of the Money, which ſhall be Subſcribed by any Perſons, Natives or Foreigners, Bodies Politick or Corporate, who are deſirous to be Subſcribers and Contributors, upon the Terms and Advantages in the ſaid Act mentioned.

Genoa, May 16. The Governor of *Milan* arrived here yeſterday, being accompanied by the Count *de Breiner,* Commiſſary-General of the Emperors Forces in *Italy*; His Excellency has been Complemented by ſix Gentlemen in the Name of the Republick, and is Lodged in the Palace of the Duke *de San Pietro*; and from hence he intends to go to *Final,* to view the Garison and Fortifications of that place. A conſiderable Supply of Money has been lately remitted hither from *Spain,* for the Service of the State of *Milan.*

Venice, May 21. The Count *de Steinau,* who is going to ſerve this Republick as General of their Land Forces in the *Levant,* deſigns to paſs thither with the next Convoy, which may be ready to ſail towards the end of this month; About which time, the Popes Gallies, and thoſe of *Malta,* are expected at *Meſſina,* where they are to join, and ſo proceed together to the *Levant.*

Turin, May 24. The Marquis *de Leganez* is come hither from *Final,* to confert with his Royal Highneſs ſeveral matters relating to the Campaigne; And to morrow his Excellency returns to *Milan*; From whence the Spaniſh Forces will now in few days begin their march towards *Piedmont.* The Vaudois defeated the laſt Week a French Party in the Valley of *St. Martin,* of whom ſeveral were killed, 22 taken, and about 70 drowned in a River which they endeavoured to paſs; and ſince that, they have cut off another French Party, that was conducting the Baggage of ſome French Officers to *Pignerol.* The French Troops are drawing together about *Suſa.*

Warſaw, May 26. The laſt Letters from the Court at *Zalkiew* give an Account, That the Treaty of Marriage between the Elector of *Bavaria* and the Princeſs of *Poland,* was concluded; and that the Baron *de Meyer,* his Electoral Highneſs's Envoy Extraordinary, was on his departure from thence, in order to his return to *Bruſſels.* The ſame Letters ſay, that the Ceremonies of the Marriage are to be performed in this City about the beginning of *Auguſt*; and that the King and Queen of *Poland* intend to accompany the Princeſs as far as *Dantzick,* where the will be received by the Ambaſſadors of his Electoral Highneſs, and conducted by Sea to *Flanders.*

Vienna, May 26. The Rendezvous of the Imperial Forces in *Hungary* is appointed to be at *Baſia* on the River *Drave,* where, as we are aſſured by the Advices from thoſe parts, the whole Army will be aſſembled by the middle of the next month; General *Caprara,* who is to command them this Compagne, is ſhortly expected from *Piedmont*; and in the mean time, General *Starenberg,* Governor of *Eſſeck,* has the care of ordering all matters, with relation to the Encamping of the Troops as they arrive, and the making the neceſſary Proviſion for them. The Letters from *Peter Waradin* Adviſe, that ſeveral Turkiſh Barks and Gallies, who are to be employed on the *Danube,* were come to *Belgrade*; That 4 or 5000 Turks were arrived in the Neighborhood of that place; and that the whole Ottoman Army would be in the Field by the end of *June.*

Hailbron, June 1. The Confederate Forces continue to draw together near this place; Moſt of the Foot lies at *Gradiſch,* and the Horſe at *Vaihingen* on the River *Ens*; Three Regiments of the Elector *Palatin*'s Troops are come to *Gundelsheim,*

two

THE FOUNDING OF THE BANK OF ENGLAND The *Gazette* for June 7–11 1694 reproduced the Order in Council instructing the Treasury to advertise in the *Gazette* Mary II's approval of the commission for founding the Bank of England.

obliges me to wait for the proof".* The enfeebled King could not stand the late hours. In July 1712 he resigned, to die in the following December.

During the last weeks of his editorship *Gazettes* had become double issues, that is four-page papers, on most publication days. This was the result of the passing in June 1712 of an Act to relieve insolvent debtors, who hitherto could be consigned to prison for small sums although they had the means to discharge a portion of their liabilities.† Among the clauses was one requiring the debtor to give notice to his creditors in the *Gazette*. Immediately it was flooded with insertions. Part of page three and all page four of no. 5014 for June 5–7 were filled with such notices and the price of 2d. was added below the imprint to inform the public of the change of size. In the following double issue the advertising flowed on to page two, making a normal issue and two pages wholly devoted to further advertising. When this occurred the price became 1d., 2d. being reserved for the four-pagers in which the buyer had a higher proportion of editorial matter.

King's place was quickly filled by another of Swift's nominees, his good friend and Irish neighbour Charles Ford. When Swift found the job for Ford he had no ambition for the *Gazette* but hoped to serve the friendship. "His salary [£200]", he told Stella, "is paid him every week if he pleases without taxes or abatements; he has little to do for it, he has a pretty office, with coals, candles, paper etc., can frank what letters he will; and his perquisites if he takes care may be worth £100 more". This was the description of a comfortable government sinecure. To Swift's irritation, "the puppy does not seem satisfied with it . . . and makes 20 difficulties", when to the benefactor it seemed "the prettiest employment in England of its bigness". To Ford the

Correspondence, undated notes, pp. 236, 237, 259.

†10 Anne c. 20. An Act for the relief of insolvent debtors by obliging their creditors to accept the utmost satisfaction they are capable to make, and restoring them to their liberty.

objection—which Hedges might have understood—was that the post "was not genteel enough".*

The Newspaper Stamp Duty

His appointment coincided with the imposition of a tax on newspapers. The instigator was St John, who sought to placate Tory extremists by abating the opposition Press, the licensing system of the sixteenth and seventeenth centuries being superseded by control through taxation. Every pamphlet or paper, including newspapers, and consisting of not more than one sheet, i.e. of four pages, was to pay $\frac{1}{2}$d. on each half sheet. The *Gazette* was not exempt and after August 1 1712 copies bore the handsome rose and thistle of the $\frac{1}{2}$d. stamp or the lion of the 1d. Most newspapers contained themselves within the half sheet and raised its price to $1\frac{1}{2}$d. The *Gazette* was because of advertising still obliged to print four-page issues but the periodicity reverted to twice-weekly.†

Under the same Act (10 Anne c. 19) advertisements were separately taxed at 1s. an insertion, an impost that had little effect on the official advertising in the *Gazette* but diminished the private appeals for stolen horses and runaway staff. By a third tax, that on paper, newspapers were further hit, These three taxes, which survived until the mid-nineteenth century, later became known as the "taxes on knowledge" for as they were successively increased to bring in revenue they crippled the production of cheap periodicals for the working class.

Initial difficulty in collecting the duties encouraged non-compliance and by 1714 newspaper proprietors had found the loophole whereby six pages were liable only to the larger pamphlet tax of 2s. on the edition. The *Gazette* with its substantial advertising easily made up six pages and so appeared unstamped.

*Swift to Stella, July 1 1712.

†*Red and Black*, an account of the duty and postage stamps impressed on newspapers 1712–1870, was printed privately by The Times Publishing Company Limited in 1962.

Charles Ford

Under Ford the *Gazette* was used as it had been in the 1710 election to prove by the documentation of loyal addresses and speeches that the public and the Crown approved Tory measures and Tory ministers, particularly the making of the peace at Utrecht. Although it was dutifully kept free from comment, it was equally with the declared ministerial Press an instrument of propaganda. As the shipping news had fallen away before the increase of proclamations and departmental paragraphs, so the foreign news lost ground to the verbiage of praise from governors of colonies, mayors and councils, justices, sheriffs, chancellors, freeholders and any body disposed to express to the Crown its gratitude for the way the country was being governed.

In his editing Ford was even more timid than Perrot. On Queen Anne's death he sent Swift the *Gazette* containing the bleak obituary, explaining that "I had writ a good deal more of the Queen's illness, an account of her birth etc. But I could not find out Mr L[ewis, the under-secretary] and had no body to consult with, and therefore chose rather to say too little, than anything I doubted might be improper".*

The death of the Queen on August 1 1714 ended the political careers of her chief minister Oxford and his associates. He was impeached and Bolingbroke evaded that fate only by flight to the Continent. The government of George I was formed of the Whigs who had summoned him from Hanover and placed him on the throne under the restraints of the Revolution of 1688. When the challenge briefly presented by the Old Pretender in "the Fifteen" collapsed the country settled down to a period of peace, prosperity and expansion such as it had not known before.

The Whigs Take Over the Gazette

Ford remained at the *Gazette* only a few weeks before his place was commandeered for a loyal Whig: Samuel Buckley, since

Letters of Jonathan Swift to Charles Ford (Oxford 1935), pp. xv and 47.

47

1703 publisher, editor and also printer of England's first, and still in 1714 only, daily newspaper, the *Courant*. Buckley's earliest editorial principle had been to avoid comment since readers could "make reflections for themselves". This highminded detachment from political controversy proved economically impossible to maintain in a non-official newspaper and he modified the *Courant* while keeping it a paper of news that was generally esteemed. A good linguist, capable of making his own translations from the foreign papers, he was a practical man, tied by experience and temperament to the printing trade and business world rather than to literary circles.

During the last reign he had served the Whigs well by two skilful "leaks" of information. On October 13 1711 the *Courant* had published the text of the peace preliminaries with France which disclosed concessions that in the Whig view betrayed allies and offered little advantage to this country. It was followed on December 5 by the text of the memorial of protest against the peace from the Elector of Hanover.

Both documents were material that had been withheld from the official newspaper since the ministry could risk the publication of neither. Had a licensing Act been in force the public would have known nothing. Not until the nineteenth century, under the leadership of *The Times*, would the right and duty of the Press to make disclosures in the public interest become established. Buckley's motive had however been to embarrass the government and he was saved by the consequences for the Tory majority in the Lords melted away and the Queen readmitted Whig advisers to her presence. When under the new King the Whigs returned to full power it was better to have Buckley on their side: he was rewarded with the *Gazette*.*

No. 5263 of the *Gazette*, September 25–28 1714, was the first prepared by the new Gazetteer and it was printed by Jacob

*See Michael Foot: *The Pen and the Sword* (1957) for a detailed account of these disclosures and their effect.

Tonson, who had lost the contract in the years of Tory triumph. He made no typographical changes and, allowing for the slight variations of design in type held by printers before the days of standardization by mechanized type-casting, the *Gazette* looked much as before. In Buckley's first numbers he was overwhelmed with the addresses and appointments of the new reign which taxed the capacity of even six-page issues and added little to the interest of the contents.

Like Steele he found the foreign correspondence difficult to organize with regularity and an unsuccessful circular soon after the accession was followed in 1718 by a more precise appeal. This began: "His Majesty has been pleased to give direction that the *London Gazette*, which is published by the Royal Authority, should for the future be regularly and sufficiently furnished with all proper advices and intelligence from abroad." The range of material, including the latest literary news, that was expected would have kept occupied an "Our Own Correspondent" of later days, and at least one flabbergasted recipient protested. He was reminded that Buckley was to have "in his hand materials not only for the *Gazette* but for other things the Government may think for its service".* As Buckley continued his *Daily Courant* the benefit of what was delivered to him by the Secretaries accrued to that paper at the expense of the bi-weeekly *Gazette*. For this he appears to have had the Government's blessing. The *Courant* was also being subsidized by official bulk buying for free distribution.†

The circulation of the *Gazette*, which due to competition steadily declined after Steele left the Secretary's office, was apparently not a matter of concern to Buckley. While bulk buying of the *Courant* increased until it reached over 2,000 a day, so the circulation of the *Gazette* remained after 1717 at less than 2,000,

---

*Both letters are printed in "The *London Gazette* in 1718: Supply of news from abroad" by Ragnild Hatton in the *Bulletin* of the Institute of Historical Research (1940–41), xviii, 108, from the Dayrolle Papers, B.M., Add. MSS., 15867, f. 36.
†See Calendar of Treasury Papers.

of which more than half represented copies distributed to officials.* In his methods Buckley was efficient rather than venal. By controlling the *Gazette* he controlled the chief competitor of the *Courant*, the paper that was close to his heart as well as his pocket. The finance and organization of a daily newspaper when hand printing restricted the number of copies to a few thousand had to have help, direct or indirect. Sales and advertising revenue were insufficient to cover costs, news was difficult and expensive to obtain.

Until 1719 the *Courant* was the sole daily but journals of less periodicity had steadily increased despite the Stamp Act. Two most successful were the *Evening Post* (founded in 1709) and the *St James's Evening Post* (1715), both thrice weekly and both a nuisance to the *Gazette* because they could filch its news and injure its sale.† A critic reproaching the government for failing to revise the Stamp Act to close the loophole of the stamp-free six-pagers, viewed the evening newspapers as interlopers of journalism, feeding richly off the publications that appeared in the morning. Buckley, who with no. 5724 of February 24 1717 had become the printer as well as the writer of the *Gazette*, defended its pages by delaying the start of printing.

In 1717 Buckley, then in his mid-forties, had confirmed to him the Gazetteership by a patent for life.‡ This innovation was a mistake. By it he was secured for the Whigs, but he no longer had the spur to carry the *Gazette* to greater heights. The ministry was well aware of the necessity of, as Harley had put it, "some discreet writer of the Government's side", but the concern was no longer to "get facts right" or even to give facts. By subsidizing writers on journals other than the *Gazette* the government achieved its end.

*J. R. Sutherland, "Circulation of Newspapers and Literary Periodicals 1700–30", *The Library*, 4th series (1934–35), xv, 110. The total profit for the period October 25 1717–December 25 1719 was £902. 12s. 5½d.

†John Toland's proposal for regulating the newspapers, B.M., Add. MSS., 4295, ff. 49–50, printed in Hanson, op. cit., pp. 135–138.

‡*Political State of Great Britain*, xvii, 652.

The service that the Crown might render to subjects, which had been the ostensible purpose of Williamson's *Gazette*, was neglected. Throughout the eighteenth century the service that the Press might render to a ministry to keep it in power was the paramount consideration in engaging in journalism. For this the *Gazette* had the limited use evolved since Williamson's day.

Both George I and George II were conscious that they had prerogative powers but they found them curtailed and were often to lament that things were better in Hanover. They had the right to appoint and dismiss ministers but their choice was being restricted to men who could find support in Parliament and they were obliged to dismiss office-holders not because they were unsatisfactory to the Crown but to Parliament. By an immense patronage, chiefly derived from posts in the household and the growing public service, the Crown exercised considerable influence on Parliament, although since Anne's reign less by placemen and more by manipulation of electors. For those involved in this sytem of favour for service rendered the *Gazette* was a working tool for it was the organ of the Crown and its servants. The number circulated in government departments outweighed those going to the public: the balance of Williamson's day was reversed.

Chapter VI 1727–1828

Sir Robert Walpole

In June 1727 George I died. George II planned, in the style of Hanoverian heirs, to bring in with him the, as it were, Shadow Cabinet of ministers he had formed in opposition during his father's lifetime. But on an accession suitable royal speeches had to be ghosted by the incoming chief minister. He helplessly asked Sir Robert Walpole, the outgoing incumbent, what should be said; and from that moment Walpole was back in the saddle. As the cynical Lord Hervey noted in his diary, recourse to back numbers of the *Gazette* would have supplied the material.

Management of the Press had become systematic under Walpole after 1721. His ministry encouraged the foundation of pro-government newspapers, paid writers and distributed free copies, spending lavishly from secret service funds until the mid-1730s when the accusations mounted by opposition papers on the outlay of public money obliged a retrenchment. Buckley, whose *Courant* had done very well until 1735, when it was consolidated with two others as a single government paper, was then in his sixties. He died on September 8 1741. Samuel Johnson, defining "Gazetteer" in his *Dictionary* published in 1755, was probably referring to Buckley when he set down the term as "lately . . . of the utmost infamy, being usually applied to wretches who were hired to vindicate the court".

Despite taxation there was an important expansion of the Press during Buckley's lifetime. On February 3 1730 no. 1 was published of a new style daily which treated advertising as main news: the *Daily Advertiser*. Its aim was to collect the insertions normally scattered among all the papers then established so that a single notice missed attention. Bankruptcies, commodity, stock and exchange prices were added, supported by a few news items. The *Daily Advertiser*, though not the first advertising sheet, was the first successfully to rest newspaper finance on advertising, which has the merit that, unlike editorial matter, it takes up paid-for space. That when the *Advertiser* was founded much editorial matter was paid for did not affect its success and influence. Within a decade all the morning papers were giving commercial intelligence and the course of the Exchange, the quotations of the public funds and market news were firm features.* The *Advertiser* extended the City news once found in the *Gazette*; it also drained off the miscellaneous advertising, such as property and auction sales, that had gone to the *Gazette*, but did not affect the official and legal insertions.

The Patent Returns to the Under-Secretary

On Buckley's death the life patent of Gazette writer at £300 a year reverted to a government official, Edward Weston, an under-secretary in the Northern Department. Born in 1703 he was the son of a Bishop of Exeter and after a few years as tutor to Lord Townshend's children he had in 1729 begun his career in the public service as under-secretary, Townshend being then Secretary for the Northern Department. Weston remained there until 1746, when he became Chief Secretary for Ireland, but was recalled in 1761 and until 1764 had a second innings as under-secretary, again for the Northern Department. His health then obliged him to retire. A classical scholar with a facility for poetic epitaphs, Weston was an agreeable but insignificant fellow, efficient enough in a post that demanded no political decisions.

Although he paid a deputy £30 to run the *Gazette*† he took

*Stanley Morison, *The English Newspaper* (Cambridge 1932), p. 127.

†*Parliamentary Papers, Reports*, x, no. 103, pp. 5–7.

pride in it and drew the attention of correspondents to it. In 1744 and 1745 friends lamented to him the lateness of its publication, which "must be a great damp to its sale", and, wrote one, "it vexes me to see your *Gazette* come out too late for the post, and yet early enough for the next day's papers to purloin your news".*

Although the *Gazette* was losing ground to the flourishing Press of the capital it still possessed, particularly abroad, an unequalled prestige and authority. After the battle of Minden on August 1 1759 French documents were seized which, so Weston was told, "open up many things of a very curious and interesting nature, particularly with regard to the French army, their views according to the various events of war, and their German connections and alliances". The King spent three days examining these papers. Publication in the *Gazette* was then resolved, "chiefly . . . to expose their cruel plans in case of success, and to open the eyes of some of the German Princes, who are treated with contempt, and merely as tools for carrying on their designs".† In such matters there was no substitute for the official authorized newspaper.

In March 1761 Lord Bute, companion, tutor and friend to George III, who had succeeded to his grandfather's throne in 1760, became Secretary for the Northern Department and, through his influence with the King, filled the vacuum created by disagreement between William Pitt (later Lord Chatham) and the Duke of Newcastle. Pitt resigned in October, Newcastle in May 1762, leaving the Scots lord in sole possession of the royal favour but without support among ministerial colleagues and fearful of the opposition of ex-ministers. To defend his policies and publicize

---

*Most of the references in the Weston Papers are complaints of the non-arrival of "your *Gazette* to which you refer" (H.M.C., 10th Report, iv, 279 and 280). Two letters from Stephen Poyntz, May 31 1744 and March 8 1745, refer to late publication.

†G. Black to Weston, October 29 1759, H.M.C., 10th Report, iv, Appendix 1, p. 319.

his case Bute set up his own newspaper, the *Briton*, of which no. 1 appeared on May 30 1762. It was edited by a fellow Scot, Tobias Smollett, then a public figure because of his much admired *History of England* and his editorship of the *Critical Review*, a literary-theatrical magazine.

Wilkes and "Liberty"

The *Briton* in no way competed with the *Gazette*, being from the first intended as propaganda and chiefly containing matter in defence of Bute. It is only remembered because it called forth John Wilkes' *North Briton*, which scathingly attacked the newcome "Scottish Interest" in public affairs and at Court. The *Briton* ceased to appear after February 12 1763, some weeks before the notorious no. 45 of April 23 1763, referring to a passage in the King's speech as a falsehood, ended the career of the *North Briton*.

As under-secretary Weston was involved in the execution of the general warrant issued by the Secretaries of State against Wilkes for the attack on the King—though not the Crown—in no. 45. This opened the long running engagement between Wilkes and the Government and Parliament in which a new slogan, "the liberty of the Press", became a rallying cry. The liberty sought was partly based on the long-standing grievance that the House of Commons did not permit reporting of debates; but chiefly sought was the freedom to abuse and attack King and ministers and any other men in public life.

There was no grievance against the *Gazette*, no demand that the official newspaper should disclose matters of public concern, no call for the Press to keep the people fully informed on matters of fact. The Mother of Parliaments was however the major institution which banned a public record of its proceedings, and the agitation of the 1760s compelled the Commons sullenly to acquiesce in Parliamentary reporting by 1771.

Many of the issues raised by Wilkes provided material for

unsigned and signed letters appearing in the Press between 1767 and 1772 contributed by "Junius", a vigorous writer whose identity has not been established. In the eleventh letter Weston was abused as a place and pension seeker, "a volunteer with the stipend of twenty commissions . . . no man is better acquainted with the bounty of government". Weston, it was thought by Junius, had defended the ministry of Lord Grafton in a pamphlet; there was no allusion to the *Gazette*. It was as though those so passionately defining the function of journalism did not hold the *Gazette* to be a newspaper.

"The Only Paper of Authority"

In 1764 Weston had collected his last pension of £750 and retired to the country where on July 15 1770 he died. A year earlier Lord Weymouth, then Secretary for the Southern Department, had issued a circular letter appealing on Weston's behalf for support from the embassies abroad because the reputation of the *Gazette* was sinking and the sale contracting on account of the small amount of foreign news it supplied. The letter was issued with the King's consent and Weymouth reminded recipients that they should take "particular care, as the *Gazette* is the only paper of authority printed in this country, never to send anything concerning which there is the smallest doubt".* The *Gazette* still maintained its standards although insistence on accuracy at the expense of punctuality was not held a virtue by the contemporary Press. An attempt to reinstate the authority and replenish the coffers came too late however to benefit the old *Gazette* writer.

In 1765 Grafton, Secretary for the Northern Department, engaged as his private secretary William Fraser at a salary of £400 a year, and shortly afterwards promoted him to under-secretary, joined in office with Edmund Burke. Fraser was further

*Circular from Lord Weymouth of July 7 1769, Calendar H.O. Papers, 1766–69, p. 483.

rewarded on July 23 1770 with the grant of *Gazette* writer for life at a salary of £270.* Like Weston Fraser was a lieutenant, careful and punctual but content to leave initiative to others.

The Heyday of Press "Management"

The grant preceded changes in journalism that were the aftermath of no. 45 and of Junius. The accession of debates in Parliament to the columns of newspapers stimulated circulations. The *Morning Post*, founded in 1772, discovered that there was a novel revenue to be obtained from bribes for puffs, or for the contradiction, suppression and insertion of what were called "personalities", paragraphs of which well-known persons were the subject. By 1780 so successful was this unsavoury forerunner of the modern gossip column that the rest of the Press was joyfully following the *Post* into lucrative corruption. Members of the Government were as eager as social celebrities to pay for favourable publicity and to buy off unfavourable, and it became part of the duties of many senior public servants to do their share of "managing" the Press by arranging for the supply of paragraphs. In this clamour Fraser conducted the *Gazette* unmoved.

The greatest of the "managers" was to be George Rose, formidable Secretary of the Treasury during both the younger Pitt's administrations. His was a political appointment: in 1782 he came in with Shelburne, in April 1783 he went out when the Fox-North coalition was formed and in December 1783 he returned under Pitt. It was in Rose's own interest to underpin by every means the ministers upon whom his career depended. Fraser, whose under-secretaryship was a permanency, was in the position of the modern senior civil servant, unaffected by the rise and fall of ministers. He stayed with the Crown, and the *Gazette* remained the official journal of record and not one of the newspapers on the Treasury leash. These varied in number between seven and nine and in most cases Rose, with his hand deep in

*Calendar H.O. Papers, 1760–65, p. 579, and 1770–72, p. 160.

secret service funds, dictated absolutely what was to be said. The opposition papers, which could look only to private subsidy, reached a maximum of seven and fell as low as three.

The distinction between the *Gazette* and other newspapers became sharper in the mid-1780s when the ambition of the Prince to displace a father of questioned sanity brought new largesse to papers that declared for Buckingham or Carlton House. In this spirit the *Daily Universal Register*, founded on January 1 1785—and in 1788 to be re-titled *The Times*—adopted on that New Year's Day a royal device: the proprietor, John Walter I, had expectations from the Treasury.

On the same day in 1785 the *Gazette* also rearranged the headpiece to include the royal coat-of-arms, appropriately adopted by the newspaper of the Crown. The opportunity was taken to transfer "Numb." to the left and to insert a folio on the right-hand top corner, consecutive pagination for the year being introduced. At this period the size varied between four (3½d.) and eight (7d.) pages. Tables of the weekly average price of corn and the returns of corn and grain were regularly inserted. These and the considerable number of notices from the public offices encroached on space once given to foreign news. Under Fraser such news dwindled to an occasional short paragraph.

Whereas the pages of other newspapers were becoming crowded owing to the pressure of news and advertising, the typography of the *Gazette* was becoming more spacious. Its page size, which had scarcely changed since 1665, was by the 1780s and 90s markedly smaller than that of the successful daily newspapers where the type area was extended to the limits that could be accommodated in the wooden hand printing press. Contemporaries were hungry for space, as are newspapers today. The *Gazette* was typographically no longer a newspaper but a handsomely laid-out journal of public announcements and advertising.

Corruption of the Press did not perturb the Commons but that of the public service did. After 1780, when John Dunning, M.P. for Calne, successfully moved the resolution that "the power of the Crown has increased, is increasing, and ought to be diminished", there were a number of attempts to limit and control patronage. Edward Burke and other members pressed for the reduction of sinecures and for the cost of government to be brought under Parliamentary control by distinguishing personal and household expenditure from the rest of the Civil List.

One measure to improve efficiency was the redefinition of the jumbled duties of the Northern and Southern Departments. On March 27 1782 the King appointed Charles Fox Foreign Secretary and Lord Shelburne Home Secretary, the old Departments becoming the Foreign and Home Offices. Sheridan, who was Fox's own manager of the Press, was briefly Fraser's colleague as one of the two Foreign Office under-secretaries, but Fraser remained as a permanency until 1789. The interest of the Northern and Southern Departments in the *Gazette* was inherited by the new Offices. The responsibilities of the Home Office were at first small, except for the supervision of prisons and the convict system: "The general business of the office is scarcely sufficient to furnish employment for the clerks at present borne upon the establishment", reported an investigating committee in 1785, but the *Gazette* was to record its specific concerns, such as the naturalization of aliens.*

Pitt, who took office in December 1783, continued to reform the government service by abolishing sinecures. In general he avoided the payment of compensation by waiting for the death of the useless office-holder. The Stationery Office, set up on August 15 1787 to supply certain government offices and eventually all with materials and equipment by central purchase,

---

*There were eleven clerks in 1785 when a Privy Council Committee investigated fees and emoluments in the public offices.

absorbed a number of sinecures, such as that of Horace Walpole, usher of the receipt of the Exchequer and supplier of stationery to the Treasury.*

Thus the modern civil service began to emerge from the trappings of fealty and patronage and top-level muddle sorted out by ill-paid underlings. The reformed service was fledgling, and burdened by superfluous departments of medieval origin staffed by only one or two clerks. At the end of the eighteenth century there were fifty-three public offices of which few had more than thirty members of staff. The Foreign Office had only two dozen as the country plunged into Continental wars, the Home Office two bakers' dozens less than a decade after the French Revolution. The two revenue departments, the hard core of the national economy, Customs and Excise, both with staffs of over 6,000, were Gullivers in the Lilliput service. In every department pluralism was rife. There were posts whose holders had not been in the building for thirty years but who drew a salary and paid a deputy. After years of Pittite reform there were still in 1810 242 sinecures costing the country nearly £300,000 a year.

Perquisites and the Gazette

Fraser himself was a pluralist. To his under-secretaryship with £500 a year and over £400 in fees, he added £270 as *Gazette* writer, £218 as Clerk of the Signet, £90 as Patent King's Waiter, £300 as German translator (though this was towards the end of his life) and £50 from miscellaneous funds. The Committee of the Privy Council instructed in 1785 to investigate fees and emoluments in public offices deprecated the employment of clerks on the *Gazette* when they had other duties assigned and recommended that the post of *Gazette* writer should be abolished. The response of the Secretaries was that the post was one of three to which they could appoint officers who deserved reward for

*Treasury Minute Books, lviii, 493–5.

diligence and long service, the other two being the admitted sinecures of the Collector and Transmitter of State Papers and the Secretary of the Latin Tongue.

As Fraser himself paid for his deputy the arrangement was allowed to continue and on January 30 1797 Stephen Rolleston, a senior clerk at the Foreign Office at a salary of £450, was formally appointed deputy writer. When Fraser died on December 11 1802 Rolleston immediately succeeded to the patent and, according to his own account, did not bring in a deputy.*

The Committee of 1785 also discovered that the clerks in the Home and Foreign Offices were accustomed to receive a number of free *Gazettes*, the private sale of which added usefully to their pay. In 1798 first the clerks in the Home Office and then those in the Foreign agreed to commute for the cash value during their tenure of office and accordingly they received some £75 each a year.† This receipt of free copies, which probably dated back at least to Buckley's day, was also shared by the office- and door-keepers but their perquisite was not withdrawn. The profits on the *Gazette* were £282 to each Office.

The Sun *and the* True Briton

Fraser was succeeded as under-secretary in 1789 by James Bland Burges, a busy, reforming fellow who supported Burke's proposal that the Government should have a newspaper in its keeping. He found Rose co-operative. John Heriot, an experienced journalist on a government-subsidized newspaper, was secured as editor and on October 1 1792 the evening *Sun* and the morning *True*

---

*At the beginning of 1799 he was promoted to second chief clerk, which carried a salary of £900 a year and on February 20 1801 a supplementary payment of £250 a year was allowed to him as assistant to the under-secretaries. By July 1806 his salary had risen to £1,250 excluding the Gazetteership. (P.R.O., F.O. Papers 366/380 and 366/413.)

†P.R.O., F.O. Papers 366/387 and the evidence of Thomas Plasket, chief clerk at the Home Office, to the investigating Committee.

Briton were launched. It is not clear whether Rose and Francis Freeling, Secretary of the Post Office, put up the capital privately, but during the founding period Freeling received several secret service payments and Rose was never anxious to use his own money.

The Treasury's support of the *True Briton* was withdrawn in 1804, when Pitt returned to office, and Heriot acquired for himself most of the shares in the more successful *Sun*; but for some ten or twelve years the two journals were in the Press what Gatton and Old Sarum were in the House of Commons. They were not to be despised for Heriot understood good writing and their organization was first-rate: the support of the Treasury ensured finance, that of the Foreign Office the dispatches, and that of the Post Office the foreign journals over the delivery of which that department kept a strict control.

The elementary method of obtaining foreign news by translating what had been published in newspapers abroad, the method of Buckley in his *Courant*, was still the practice. As in the days of Muddiman, all letters passed through the General Post Office, as it had become, and the clerks were able to control the delivery of packets of such journals, easily recognizable because of the characteristic newspaper format. They guarded a lucrative monopoly: that of supplying translations themselves from journals they obtained. They had the power to hold the newspaper proprietors up to ransom; and did. Hence the importance to the *Sun* of the connection with Freeling. By the end of the eighteenth century the *Gazette* was printing no foreign news except that on the war. So it was losing its importance as a paper of current news.

The Times *becomes Independent*

Between 1805 and 1807 the Post Office monopoly was broken by *The Times*, then under the energetic direction of John Walter II, son of the founder, after exhausting years of hide and seek with the omnipotent clerks. The struggle was undertaken by Walter because he wished not only to have free access to foreign journals but to employ his own correspondents. In the past newspapers had received letters from occasional agents but there had been no systematic coverage such as that available to the *Gazette* through the embassies abroad. Walter usurped the supremacy the *Gazette* had once enjoyed. During the blockade of the Continent after 1809 he continually anticipated the Government and the Post Office since he employed his own blockade runner to land dispatches at lonely coves where horsemen were waiting to carry them direct to the office of *The Times*. There were several occasions in the last years of the Napoleonic wars when he was able to give the latest news to departments of State. On others he reprinted the extraordinaries of the *Gazette*, as in a special second issue of *The Times* on June 22 1815 which gave the news of the Battle of Waterloo.

Public appreciation of Walter's policy of independent and exclusive news was reflected by a rise in circulation that strained to the limit the production of the hand presses of *The Times*. To increase the printing run Walter sponsored the steam press invented by Friedrich Koenig and his associate Andreas Bauer. The issue of *The Times* for November 29 1814 was the first printed matter to come from the press at a speed of 1,100 impressions an hour. This was the beginning of a revolution in periodical publishing, and in the concept of the freedom of the Press and the place of the newspaper in public life.

Massive production and circulation that for many years was confined to a single newspaper inevitably drew to its columns the bulk of the advertising then available. Increased revenue from this source made Walter independent of subsidies or fees and he joined independent news and independent comment. Hitherto an editor had had limited powers of rejection and selection and arrangement of items; in 1817 Walter appointed a true Editor, responsible for policy. For the first time a newspaper could assess all government action by the sole criterion of the public interest. For more than a quarter of a century *The Times* maintained a unique position in the British Press, rich, free, and in terms of circulation supreme.

The rise of *The Times*, embracing the duties of vigilance and the enlightenment of public opinion, completed the decline as a newspaper of the *Gazette*, begun in 1694–95, carried forward by the government-supported newspapers, assisted by the contraction of the prerogative. Rolleston, unlike his predecessors, was never an under-secretary: until 1817 he was not even a chief clerk, and this was during a period when the senior posts in the expanding civil service were gathering an importance and responsibility denied to Weston and his contemporaries.

The "New Establishment"

Since 1798 the printing had been executed by the then King's Printer, Andrew Strahan, whose house was near Gough Square, off Fleet Street. As the Continental war continued the number of extraordinary issues of the *Gazette* exposed the inconvenience of printing so far from Whitehall. The contract was due to expire in 1811 and Rolleston was instructed to find more suitable premises. In December 1811 he reported that he had taken a 12-year lease on 46 Parliament Street at a rent of £200. Fifteen rooms were available for editing, printing and publishing and some spare rooms were used by Rolleston. This arrangement for housing the *Gazette* under one roof came to be known as the "New Establishment". The profits for a quarter bought all the equipment including type and nine hand presses.*

*The presses were, according to Rolleston, "a new mode of printing", devised "after a plan suggested by me, and carried into execution under my direction," which halved the number of presses Strahan had used. In the absence of further detail it is impossible to decide what sort of press a Foreign Office clerk could devise that superseded the equipment of the King's Printer. However eight were still in existence in 1842 when the Comptroller of the Stationery Office found them in very bad condition and of a description long since banished from all the best printing offices" (McCulloch writing on March 12 1842, P.R.O., H.O. Papers, 45 OS 368). They had stood up creditably since 1811 to the heavy pressure of *Gazette* printing. (P.R.O., F.O. Papers, 366/413.)

The mechanical side was placed in the charge of Robert G. Clarke as *Gazette* printer appointed by the Foreign Office. He was at the time editor of the *Sun* and a government place was the customary method of acknowledging a loyal journalist's service.* The post was subordinate to the *Gazette* writer although they shared responsibility for accounts. At this time the *Gazette* was ranging in size between 14 pages (price 2s.) to 28 pages (price 3s. 6d.), owing to the amount of government information, including regular commodity and financial tables and announcements of war contracts. The first number printed by Clarke, the issue of September 28–October 1 1811, was distinguished by typographical changes that reflected the current fashion for contrast between intense black and white, but the layout of the pages remained as spacious as in the 1790s.

In September 1817 Rolleston succeeded to the chief clerkship where he remained until his retirement at the end of 1823. By then the number of clerks at the Foreign Office had increased from eight to eighteen, one of them being in attendance on himself, and his salary had increased to £1,811. His son Henry, who was translator for the German language, assisted him with the *Gazette* until the patent expired on his death on November 19 1828.

*P.R.O., F.O. Papers, 366/413, Lord Wellesley to Clarke, July 18 1811; A. Aspinall, *Politics and the Press c. 1780–1850* (1949).

Chapter VII 1828–45

Paper War for Patronage

On Rolleston's death Robert Peel, the Home Secretary, asserted the right of the Home Office in alternation to the appointment and supported his claim by urging the intimate connection that had grown up between the Home Office and the *Gazette*: "By far the largest proportion of public documents sent to the *Gazette* are sent from the Home Office." Lord Aberdeen, then Foreign Secretary, was not prepared to yield the patronage of his department and a lively and prolonged duel by correspondence followed. The matter was complicated by recollections that Lord Pelham, Home Secretary in 1802, had been the instrument of Rolleston's appointment; that the Home Office had usurped other appointments that should have been alternate; that Fraser had been an under-secretary in the Northern Department which became the Home Office; that Fraser as under-secretary had dealt with foreign affairs. Everyone still alive with memories of those days was asked to put pen to paper in support of one side or the other and the two Secretaries themselves exchanged characteristically vigorous letters.* Aberdeen lost and the appointment for life of William Gregson as writer and compiler at £300 a year was made by Peel.†

Among the applicants that a successful Aberdeen might have considered was Lewis Hertslet, Foreign Office librarian since

*P.R.O., F.O. Papers, 366/413.

†Rolleston's lease of 46 Parliament Street was assigned to Gregson. (P.R.O., H.O. Papers, 45 OS 2323.)

1811. Hertslet was eager to rescue "the appointment of *Gazette* writer from the degenerated condition into which it has fallen, of being in reality little short of a sinecure" and to make the *Gazette* itself "the official journal of the British Government and the only authentic channel in the kingdom for state intelligence of a political and commercial nature". Compared with the official journals of the European Powers it was inferior, not to say insignificant. He found it overloaded with proclamations, royal speeches and appointments, and wished to see in it Parliamentary Papers, Acts, foreign laws and dispatches and, in general, a greater range of material, published more frequently at a lower price. Gregson had no such ambitions.

Palmerston and the Gazette

In November 1828, when Hertslet prepared his memorandum on the *Gazette*,* its circulation fluctuated between 460 and 600, of which 173 copies were distributed free. He gave the average profits to the Foreign Office since the New Establishment as £5,500, but the figure for 1826 was nearly £11,000 and this was to remain the level, representing all but a fraction of the total fee fund of that Office.

Palmerston, who succeeded Aberdeen in 1830, took a keen interest although—or because—the *Gazette* writer was a Home Office appointee. He could not implement some of Hertslet's proposals—the Parliamentary printing, for instance, was distributed among patentees—but he noted on a memorandum referring to the discontinued foreign news that "I quite approve of the suggestion of making the *Gazette* more frequently the organ of the Government for the communication of information to the Public".† The last document not connected with military affairs had appeared in December 1813; thirty years later Palmerston's department was in active contact with Gregson

*Hertslet's memorandum of November 27 1828, P.R.O., F.O. Papers, 366/413.

†Note by Palmerston, September 13 1834, P.R.O., F.O. Papers, 366/413.

about the gazetting of treaties and commissions and similar material formally notified to the Crown by foreign Powers.

As a Foreign Secretary who lost no opportunity to affirm the prestige of the Foreign Office at its perhaps most splendid period he was sensitive to the traditional association with the *Gazette*. In political life he was an experienced manager of the Press, one more subtle than Rose for the subsidies were no longer so effective as they had been and the release or withholding of information was a secret of government manipulation. In 1834, when *The Times* denied that it had solicited information from the Foreign Office, that paper declared: "Our own information was earlier and surer, and . . . it would not consist with the pride and independence of our journal to wait for a dole of daily intelligence at public offices."* Such a statement could then be made by no other newspaper. Nor did it suit Palmerston that it should be made; to him newspapers were a weapon of politics. Yet he limited his interest in the *Gazette* to that proper to a minister of the Crown. It consequently remained "insipid".

Under Acts of 1810 and 1816 Parliament had taken responsibility for the salaries of all public officials and the second Act† marks the beginning of the true Civil Service of today, when departments instead of being servants of ministers are servants of the Crown. Not until 1834 were sinecures weeded out and no longer was it possible for a patentee to appoint a deputy. Every office by that year had a useful duty which the holder executed under Treasury regulation.‡ Gregson was therefore an active *Gazette* writer, but very much on his own in Parliament Street and with no departmental head to energize those who were responsible for his supply of intelligence. The Foreign and Home Offices received the fees but had no explicit responsibility for overall contents.

*The Times, December 26 1834.

†56 Geo. III c. 46.

‡Emmeline W. Cohen, *The Growth of the British Civil Service* (1941).

Perquisites in 1836

On November 3 1836 the Treasury appointed a committee to report on the progress made since 1785 on the abolition of fees. The evidence revealed that the 1798 commutation of the clerks' perquisite of free *Gazettes* had not extended to the lower echelons of the Foreign, Home and Colonial Offices, and that under Clarke some 150 copies of each issue were being published for the benefit of seven minor civil servants. By "ancient custom" the office- and door-keepers of the Foreign and Home Offices sold cut-price copies that had been delivered to them free, a perquisite assumed by their opposite numbers at the Colonial Office when it was separately established in 1801. Because this sale had interfered with Clarke's own he had offered to pay money, the *Gazettes* remaining at Parliament Street and being sold by himself at a penny or so more than he gave the office-keepers. This private arrangement had been continued by Francis Watts when in September 1836 the publishing was separated from the printing, which Clarke retained.*

By 1836 this arrangement was netting a useful sum for the year saw the first "mania" of railway investment to the extent of nearly £23 million. Each company had to obtain its powers by private Act of Parliament, and such Acts being notified in the *Gazette*, a backlog of advertising made daily publication necessary. Clarke's burden had to be shared. According to Watts, when he gave evidence, everything brought by individuals, solicitors and agents had to be examined "to ascertain if it be proper to go into the *Gazette*, and questions of some nicety occasionally happen with respect to the matters sought to be published". Officially he worked 8–10 hours a day, but the influx of railway advertising

*First Report of the Committee appointed by the Lords Commissioners of His Majesty's Treasury to Enquire into the Fees and Emoluments of Public Offices. Ordered by the House of Commons to be Printed March 23 1837.

The *Gazette* for September 16 1836 was "Printed at the office, in Cannon Row, Parliament Street, by Robert George Clarke of the same place, and published at the office aforesaid by Francis Watts of no. 40 Vincent Square".

often kept him busy till midnight, overtime for which he was paid no extra.

On Clarke's death in 1839 Watts considerably improved his position by obtaining his appointment as Superintendent, Printer and Publisher. As Superintendent his salary was £300, he received £150 as senior clerk for taking advertisements and as Publisher he received a guinea an issue, which brought in over £120 a year: a total of £570. From the private sale of the office-keepers' *Gazettes* he made over £200 a year and he pocketed a further £400 in trade allowances, various small sums from the sale of indexes and back numbers—which he regarded as a perquisite—and the fees he charged for examining and authenticating advertisements, for drawing up insertions and for providing certificates that advertisements had been duly published.

Thus at the peak of the railway "mania" in 1845–47 he was doing extremely well. He was however working at full stretch. The issue of November 15 1845 contained 584 pages and this was at a period when, owing to railway promotion, publishing of the *Gazette* was daily. As 2s. 8d. was the fixed maximum price the mammoth issues cost the public no more than any issue over 28 pages, the cost of production being offset by the revenue from advertising.

The Committee of 1836 reprobated his practice of commuting *Gazettes* but the Treasury took no action until after the appointment in 1840 of Charles Trevelyan as Assistant Secretary. He was to be the architect of the reforms effected in the Civil Service by Gladstone as Chancellor of the Exchequer and First Lord of the Treasury. Both men believed in reform from the top by the appointment of educated and distinguished officers whose claims rested on merit, not upon birth and patronage.

John Ramsay McCulloch
At the Stationery Office Trevelyan found already installed a

remarkable Comptroller, as the head was then known, John Ramsay McCulloch, a Scot with a considerable reputation as a writer and lecturer upon political economy both at Edinburgh and London. As well as producing treatises, essays and books, he had contributed to the *Scotsman* and for two years had been its editor, and he had also written for the *Edinburgh Review*. For a man of his range of experience, his patience with detail and definition, respected for his theories on wages and free trade, the position at the Stationery Office, to which he was appointed in 1838, offered financial security and the freedom to pursue his studies.

The post nevertheless interested him and he conscientiously discharged it, becoming vehement on such trivia as the superior eraser demanded by the Foreign Office and the quality, too high in his opinion, of books supplied to convict schools. The Stationery Office was the warehouse of the Civil Service, not only a Johnny-come-lately but a skivvy for all government departments.

Chapter VIII 1847–67

The Stationery Office investigates the Gazette

As Comptroller McCulloch supervised the printing and
publishing accounts of the *Dublin Gazette*, a publication separate
from that of London and printed under a patent, and in 1847 the
accounts of the *Edinburgh Gazette*, also separate, came under his
notice on the expiration of the current patent. He offered
suggestions to Trevelyan on the Scottish journal's future
organization, and Treasury minute of June 20 1848, approving
his proposals, was accompanied by a letter from Trevelyan asking
that the *London Gazette* should be investigated. "With respect to
the *London Gazette* we know as little here as you know at the
Treasury or less", replied the Comptroller on June 26 1848.
A second Treasury minute of August 8 1848 directed that the
London journal's accounts should in future be seen by the
Stationery Office and that after the end of the current financial
year the profits were no longer to be paid to the Home and
Foreign Offices but to the Exchequer. Under this minute
McCulloch's right was strengthened to investigate matters about
which successive Home and Foreign Secretaries had been
uninterested, the Treasury ignorant and the Stationery Office
powerless.

Watts had been frank with the 1836 Committee and
McCulloch soon knew what had happened since to improve the
Superintendent's fortunes. The least acceptable practice was the
resale of free copies. "It is indispensable in any new arrangement
of the *Gazette*", he advised the Treasury, "that this system should

be put an end to."* In general he did not object to Watts being paid; he wanted to regularize the heading under which the payment was made.

Apart from an improved system of accounting he recommended to the Treasury that the printing of the *Gazette* should be put up for competitive tender.† Trevelyan agreed and the contract was appropriately won by Harrison and Sons of St Martin's Lane, who between 1756 and 1790 had been the *Gazette*'s printers during the early years of the firm's foundation. Under the contract the printer was to provide accommodation for the clerical staff and for stock, and the *Gazette* was to be printed apart from his other work.‡ Watts remained as Superintendent at a salary of £1,200, some £500 of which McCulloch regarded as compensation for the loss of perquisites.

Trevelyan did not accept another proposal of McCulloch's, that the writership should be abolished, although in connection with the *Dublin Gazette* he was to remark: "I suppose that any respectable printer might be trusted to edit a *Gazette* which is a mere collection of official documents." In this case McCulloch disagreed, probably because in Dublin there was no equivalent for Watts: it would be "rash in the extreme", error might have serious consequences.§ Clarke had been subordinate to Rolleston but Watts dominated the scene by 1850 and when in July he let through an error in a solicitor's notice McCulloch defined "the duty of a *Gazette* Editor" as twofold: responsibility for

*S.O. Letterbooks, McCulloch to Treasury, September 21 1848.

†S.O. Letterbooks, McCulloch to Treasury, September 21 1848. He proposed three alternatives: that the *Gazette* should be printed at Government expense, the writer being abolished and the superintendent's salary increased; the sale of the Parliament Street establishment to Watts, who should then contract to print at a fixed price; the competitive tender, which he favoured.

‡Under the new contract the *Gazette* was printed by steam. McCulloch, arranging for the compensation of ten pressmen, noted on January 11 1849 that "the *Gazette* has for some time been the only paper in London printed by the hand press". The contract took effect from January 1.

§Trevelyan to McCulloch, June 1 1850, and McCulloch to Trevelyan, June 3.

acceptance or rejection, and accurate printing. He did not mention the writer.*

A Proposal to Amalgamate the Official Gazettes

In 1848 and 1851 the Scottish radical M.P., Joseph Hume, who had a formidable record of success in the reform of public administration, pressed for the *Gazette* to be made more informative and more economic. One ambition was to see Acts printed in it. Under the patent held by Eyre and Spottiswoode, the then Queen's Printers, the current term of which was not due to expire until 1860, this was impossible, but McCulloch, who for the next decade was to mount a relentless attack on the patentees, suggested that the Treasury should buy them out. He was at first inclined to reject another proposal from Hume, that the three official *Gazettes* should be amalgamated. That of Scotland he held to be necessary because "the law of Scotland is altogether peculiar"; so was the journal of Dublin owing to the barrier of the Irish Sea. "A project of this sort is, if anything can be, a burlesque not only upon economy but upon common sense," he concluded.†

Once the accounts of the three *Gazettes* were transferred to the supervision of the Stationery Office they received annual publicity on their presentation to Parliament. The cost of running the *Edinburgh Gazette* was high and that of Dublin was low: the pressure for their amalgamation with London continued. McCulloch in 1851 still demurred: "The validity of innumerable acts in civil life, the conditions in hosts of contracts, leases, etc., and (for Scotland at least) the rules of procedure in the Courts of Law etc. etc., is made to depend on references to them; or on their insertion in the *Edinburgh* and *Dublin Gazettes*." In 1852 his dissatisfaction with the Edinburgh printer outweighed his loyalty to Scotland and he yielded. A bill was drafted; but the

*McCulloch to Trevelyan, July 3 1850.

†McCulloch to Trevelyan, November 27 1848.

Edinburgh printer had influential friends and the project bore no fruit.*

The Selling Price is Lowered

Radical pressure continued. McCulloch prepared to resist a reduction in the selling price of the *London Gazette* to meet the desire that it should be more generally available and to anticipate criticism that the profits were too high. He objected: "If the *Gazette* were mine I would not touch it—I am satisfied that no reduction of price, unless you were to give it away gratis, would very materially increase its sale. . . . It is only taken by those that cannot help it."† He was however overruled. By Treasury minute of February 10 1852 the maximum price was from April 1 reduced to 1s. and this applied to all issues of eight or more pages, whereas formerly the graduated scale had risen to 2s. 8d. for all issues of over 28 pages.

That the Comptroller had been overridden was long remembered in the Stationery Office. His protests, however well grounded, were those of an economist. The Treasury action was politically expedient, a yielding to the outcry of Members such as Bright, Cobden and Hume for the relief of the working classes from the "taxes on knowledge" and for the cheap dissemination of information. The outcry was primarily directed against the newspaper stamp, into which a Parliamentary Committee enquired in 1851. Within four years the tax originally imposed in 1712 was to be repealed.

*McCulloch to Trevelyan, April 8 1851. The publicity given to the accounts may have caused him to waver, but in 1852 he was incensed by the insertion in the *Edinburgh Gazette* of the jurors' awards at the Great Exhibition. The list made 138 folio pages and the heavy cost of printing was not offset by the sale of extra copies. On May 3 1852 he suggested to Trevelyan that a short Act might be passed to give the *London Gazette* the same validity as that conferred by the *Edinburgh Gazette*, the latter journal being then suppressed. McCulloch's successor believed that the amalgamation failed because of the printer's influence, see W. R. Greg, S.O. Letterbooks, May 9 1870.

†McCulloch to Trevelyan, January 1 1852.

Numb. 10854.

The London Gazette.

Published by Authority.

From Tuesday July 26, to Saturday July 30, 1768.

Stockholm, July 12.

THE Queen of Sweden gave a magnificent Entertainment on Wednesday last to the Prince Royal, upon Occasion of his Name-Day. The Garden of Dronningholm was finely illuminated, and the Royal Family supped under a Tent, in which were placed five Tables of eight Covers each; and the whole was not ended till Two o'Clock the next Morning.

Yesterday Count Wrede Sparre was made President of the College of War. The same Day Count Zinzendorff, the Saxon Minister, arrived here from Dresden.

AT the Court at St. James's, the 29th Day of June, 1768,

PRESENT,

The KING's most Excellent Majesty in Council.

IT having been represented to His Majesty, that several Persons, who have obtained Orders of His Majesty in Council for Grants of Land in His Majesty's Island of St. John in North America, have neglected to take out such Orders, or, if taken out, to present them to His Majesty's Governor of Nova Scotia, by Means whereof His Majesty's Gracious Intentions, with Respect to the Settlement of that Island, may be defeated, and the Cultivation and Improvement thereof greatly obstructed and retarded; It is therefore this Day ordered by His Majesty in Council, that the Governor, or Commander in Chief for the Time being, of His Majesty's Colony of Nova Scotia, do forbear to pass any Grants, under the Seal of that Colony, of any Lots or Parcels of Land in His Majesties said Island of St. John, unless His Majesty's Order in Council, directing the same, shall have been produced to him on or before the first Day of May, which shall be in the Year 1769: And that this His Majesty's Order in Council be published in the London Gazette, to the End that all Persons concerned may have due Notice thereof.   *Steph. Cottrell.*

London, July 30, 1768.

THE Elector of Palatine's Minister at this Court has received Orders from his most Serene Electoral Highness, to acquaint the Merchants concerned in the Quicksilver-Trade, that one Mosengeil, Master of the Quicksilver Mines in that Electorate, having had the Assurance, from his own Accord, to sell that Commodity

[Price Three-Pence.]

in Holland and England for four Years to come, free of all Charges to Amsterdam, at 73 Kreutzers per lb. has of late absconded. As the Quicksilver from that Electorate, at future Sales, might, by that Means, fall in Price; and as the said Mosengeil was never authorised to do so; this is to caution the Traders not to make any Advances to the said Mosengeil upon such Contracts.

Pay-Office, Horse Guards, July 30, 1768.

The Right Honorable the Paymaster General of His Majesty's Forces having ordered Six Months Half-Pay to be issued to all the Reduced Officers of His Majesty's Land Forces, from the 25th of December, 1767, to the 24th of June, 1768; also Six Months Allowance to the Officers and Private Gentlemen of His Majesty's late Third and Fourth Troops of Horse Guards to the same Time: Notice is hereby declared, that on Monday next the 1st of August, Attendance will be given at the aforesaid Office for Payment of the same accordingly.
Robert Randoll.

Whitehall, July 30, 1768.

Whereas it has been humbly represented to the King, That her Grace the Dutchess of Northumberland received, on Friday the 11th of March last, at her Grace's House at Charing-Cross, in a Cover, directed as hereunder, and which had the Marks of the General Post Offices both of Dublin and London upon it, a threatening Letter, containing the Words, Letters, and Figures following, viz.

Post-Mark.   " To
DUBLIN   " Her Grace the Dutchs. of
                        " Northumber
                        " land
                        " Northumberland House
                        " London

                        " Dublin March 1st. 1768
" May it please Your Grace
        " If you do not leave two Hundred Guineas
" in a Bank Note at the Bar of the Bedford Coffee
" House directed for Mr. P. D. you may expect
" to hear of it in a dreadful Manner I hope my
" Poverty will excuse this. Though I date this
" from Dublin, Yet will I be over along with it
" and give you warning not to trifle with me for
" I shall find means to come very near yr. Person
" And shall know whether you deal Candidly
" with me or not. Please to leave the Above as
" directed on the 1st of April next, otherwise abide
" the Consequences
                        " Yours   P. D. "

And whereas it has also been represented to the King, that her said Grace the Dutchess of Northumberland has, since the Time of receiving the aforesaid threatening Letter, received two other threatening Letters,

The London Gazette.

Published by Authority.

From Monday, Septemb. 3. to Monday, Septemb. 10. 1666.

White-Hall, Sept. 8.

THe ordinary course of this Paper having been interrupted by a Sad and Lamentable Accident of Fire lately hapned in the City of *London* : It hath been thought fit for satisfying the minds of so many of His Majesties good Subjects, who must needs be concerned for the Issue of so great an Accident, to give this short, but true Accompt of it.

On the Second instant at One of the Clock in the Morning, there hapned to break out a Sad & Deplorable Fire, in *Pudding-Lane* neer *New Fish-Street*, which falling out at that hour of the night, and in a quarter of the Town so close built with wooden pitched houses, spread it self so far before day, and with such distraction to the Inhabitants and Neighbours, that care was not taken for the timely preventing the farther diffusion of it by pulling down houses, as ought to have been ; so that this lamentable Fire in a short time became too big to be mastered by any Engines or working neer it. It fell out most unhappily too, That a violent Easterly Wind fomented it, and kept it burning all that day, and the night following spreading it self up to *Grace-Church-street*, and downwards from *Cannon-street* to the Water-side as far as the *Three Cranes in the Vintry*.

The People in all parts about it distracted by the vastness of it, and their particular care to carry away their Goods, many attempts were made to prevent the spreading of it, by pulling down Houses, and making great Intervals, but all in vain, the Fire seising upon the Timber and Rubbish, and so continuing it self, even through those spaces, and raging in a bright Flame all Monday and Tuesday, notwithstanding His Majesties own, and His Royal Highness's indefatigable and personal pains to apply all possible remedies to prevent it, calling upon and helping the people with their Guards; and a great number of Nobility and Gentry unweariedly assisting therein, for which they were requited with a thousand blessings from the poor distressed people. By the favour of God the Wind slackned a little on Tuesday night, and the Flames meeting with Brick-buildings at the Temple, by little and little it was observed to lose its force on that side ; so that on Wednesday morning we began to hope well, and his Royal Highness never dispairing or slackning his Personal Care, wrought so well that day, assisted in some parts by the Lords of the Council before and behind it, that a stop was put to it at the *Temple-Church*, neer *Holborn-Bridge*, *Pie-Corner*, *Aldersgate*, *Cripple-gate*, neer the lower end of *Coleman-street*, at the end of *Basing-Hall-street*, by the *Postern*, at the upper end of *Bishopsgate street*, and *Leaden-Hall-street*, at the Standard in *Cornhill*, at the Church in *Fan-Church-street*, neer *Clothworkers-hall* in *Mincing-Lane*, at the middle of *Mark-Lane*, and at the *Tower-Dock*.

On Thursday by the blessing of God it was wholly beat down and ex inguished ; but so as that Evening it unhappily burst out afresh at the *Temple*, by the falling of some sparks (as is supposed) upon a Pile of Wooden Buildings, but his Royal Highness, who watched there that whole night in Person, by the great Labours and Diligence used, and especially by applying Powder to blow up the Houses about it, before day most happily mastered it.

Divers Strangers, *Dutch* and *French*, were, during the Fire, apprehended, upon suspition that they contributed mischievously to it, who are all imprisoned, and Informa-

tions prepared to make a severe Inquisition thereupon by my Lord Chief Justice *Keeling*, assisted by some of the Lords of the Privy Council, and some principal Members of the City ; notwithstanding which suspicions, the manner of the burning all along in a Train, and so blown forwards in all its way by strong Winds, makes us conclude the whole was an effect of an unhappy chance, or to speak better, the heavy hand of God upon us for our Sins, shewing us the terrour of his Judgment in thus raising the fire ; and immediately after, his miraculous and never enough to be acknowledged Mercy, in putting a stop to it, when we were in the last despair, and that all attempts for the quenching it, however industriously pursued, seemed insufficient. His Majesty then sat hourly in Council, and ever since hath continued making rounds about the City in all parts of it where the danger and mischief was greatest, till this Morning that he hath sent his Grace the Duke of *Albemarle*, whom he hath called for to assist him in this great occasion, to put his Happy and Succesful Hand to the finishing this memorable Deliverance.

About the *Tower*, the seasonable Orders given for plucking down Houses to secure the Magazins of Powder, was more especially succesful, that Part being up the Wind, notwithstanding which, it came almost to the very Gates of it, so as by this early provision, the severall Stores of War lodged in the Tower were entirely saved : And we have further this infinite cause particularly to give God thanks that the fire did not happen in any of those places where his Majesties Naval Stores are kept, so as though it hath pleased God to visit us with his own hand, he hath not, by disfurnishing us with the means of carrying on the War, subjected us to our Enemies.

It must be observed, That this Fire happened in a part of the Town, where though the Commodities were not very rich, yet they were so bulky, that they could not well be removed, so that the Inhabitants of that part where it first began have sustained very great loss : But by the best Enquiry we can make, the other parts of the Town, where the Commodities were of greater value , took the Alarm so early, that they saved most of their Goods of value, which possibly may have diminished the loss; though some think, that if the whole industry of the Inhabitants had been applyed to the stopping of the Fire, and not to the saving of their particular Goods, the success might have been much better, not only to the Publick, but to many of them in their own Particulars.

Through this sad Accident it is easie to be imagined how many persons were necessitated to remove themselves and Goods into the open Fields, where they were forced to continue some time, which could not but work compassion in the beholders; but His Majesties Care was most Signal in this occasion, who, besides his Personal Pains, was frequent in Consulting all wayes for relieving those distressed persons, which produced so good effect, aswell by His Majesties Proclamations, and the Orders issued to the Neighbour Justices of the Peace to encourage the sending in Provisions to the Markets, which are publickly known, as by other Directions, that when His Majesty, fearing lest other Orders might not yet have been sufficient, had Commanded the Victualler of his Navy to send Bread into *Moor-Fields* for the relief of the Poor, which for the more speedy supply, he sent in Baskets out of the Sea Stores ; it was found that the Markets had

Qqqq   been

THE GREAT FIRE OF LONDON Described in *Gazette* Numb. 85, September 3–10, printed in the Savoy where Newcomb moved after the Fire destroyed his premises at Baynard's Castle.

Numb. 17028.

The London Gazette
EXTRAORDINARY.

Publiſhed by Authority.

THURSDAY, JUNE 22, 1815.

Downing-Street, June 22, 1815.

MAJOR the Honourable H. Percy arrived late last night with a dispatch from Field-Marshal the Duke of Wellington, K. G. to Earl Bathurst, His Majesty's Principal Secretary of State for the War Department, of which the following is a copy:

My LORD, *Waterloo, June 19, 1815.*

BUONAPARTE having collected the 1st, 2d, 3d, 4th, and 6th corps of the French army and the Imperial Guards, and nearly all the cavalry on the Sambre, and between that river and the Meuse, between the 10th and 14th of the month, advanced on the 15th and attacked the Prussian posts at Thuin and Lobez, on the Sambre, at daylight in the morning.

I did not hear of these events till the evening of the 15th, and I immediately ordered the troops to prepare to march; and afterwards to march to their left, as soon as I had intelligence from other quarters to prove that the enemy's movement upon Charleroy was the real attack.

The enemy drove the Prussian posts from the Sambre on that day; and General Zieten, who commanded the corps which had been at Charleroy, retired upon Fleurus; and Marshal Prince Blucher concentrated the Prussian army upon Sombref, holding the villages in front of his position of St. Amand and Ligny.

The enemy continued his march along the road from Charleroy towards Bruxelles, and on the same evening, the 15th, attacked a brigade of the army of the Netherlands, under the Prince de Weimar, posted at Frasne, and forced it back to the farmhouse on the same road, called Les Quatre Bras.

The Prince of Orange immediately reinforced this brigade with another of the same division, under General Perponcher, and in the morning early regained part of the ground which had been lost, so as to have the command of the communication leading from Nivelles and Bruxelles, with Marshal Blucher's position.

In the mean time I had directed the whole army to march upon Les Quatre Bras, and the 5th division under Lieutenant-General Sir Thomas Picton, arrived at about half past two in the day, followed by the corps of troops under the Duke of Brunswick, and afterwards by the contingent of Nassau.

At this time the enemy commenced an attack upon Prince Blucher with his whole force, excepting the 1st and 2d corps; and a corps of cavalry under General Kellerman, with which he attacked our post at Les Quatre Bras.

The Prussian army maintained their position with their usual gallantry and perseverance, against a great disparity of numbers, as the 4th corps of their army, under General Bülow, had not joined, and I was not able to assist them as I wished, as I was attacked myself, and the troops, the cavalry in particular, which had a long distance to march, had not arrived.

We maintained our position also, and completely defeated and repulsed all the enemy's attempts to get possession of it. The enemy repeatedly attacked us with a large body of infantry and cavalry, supported by a numerous and powerful artillery; he made several charges with the cavalry upon our infantry, but all were repulsed in the steadiest manner. In this affair His Royal Highness the Prince of Orange, the Duke of Brunswick, and Lieutenant-General Sir Thomas Picton, and Major-

THE BATTLE OF WATERLOO The victory announced in the *Gazette* Extraordinary of June 22 1815.

JOHN RAMSAY MCCULLOCH
Comptroller of the Stationery Office
1838–64.

WILLIAM RATHBONE GREG
Comptroller of the Stationery Office
1864–77.

THOMAS DIGBY PIGOTT
Controller of the Stationery Office
1877–1905.

NORMAN GIBBS SCORGIE
Deputy Controller of the Stationery
Office 1919-42 and Controller 1942-49.

The Crimean War

Meanwhile the hope that a lower price would stimulate the circulation of the *Gazette* was disappointed. During 1853 the circulation remained at 350–400 copies and McCulloch gloomily pointed out to James Wilson, M.P. and Financial Secretary of the Treasury that "this measure occasioned a dead loss to government ... of £2,059. 6s. 4½d. I predicted this result".* It was not a tinkering with the selling price but the Crimean War that in 1854 was to lift the circulation—without much gain to revenue from sales. The effect of the war on other newspaper circulations was more sensational. All London's daily newspapers by the 1850s numbered their circulations in thousands and *The Times*—alone—in tens of thousands. The eminence reached by this journal was resented by successive ministries and the support given by the Government to the repeal of the stamp Act in 1855 was not a high-minded concern for the working classes so much as a vicious attack on the supremacy of a newspaper that claimed the right of disclosure in the public interest.

The heart of the repeal was that it withdrew the privilege of free postage, as valuable to nineteenth-century newspapers as it had been to Muddiman. *The Times*, bulked out as no other newspaper was by inclusive foreign and home news, Parliamentary and law reports, book reviews and other services as well as by massive advertising, was penalized by a postage based on weight. The choice for the then proprietor, John Walter III, was to keep up the price or to sacrifice the range of contents. He chose the former course and thereafter although *The Times* maintained circulation it no longer commanded a numerical superiority as the cheaper, slighter newspapers raced towards mass circulations.

In 1855 Trevelyan saw the fruition of his plan, worked out in association with Sir Stafford Northcote, for a reformed civil

---

*S.O. Letterbooks, May 18 1853. The net profit of the *Gazette* in 1851 was £9,292. 1s. 9d. and in 1852 £8,418. 7s. 11d.

service under a Commission appointed by Order in Council and recruiting its members by competitive examination.* Its progress was accelerated by the Crimean War which laid bare the defects of the old system of birth and patronage. The suffering of our troops, ill-clad, ill-fed, disease-wasted and disorganized in the bitter weather of the peninsula, and the blundering of officialdom that had led to disasters such as the charge of the Light Brigade, were relentlessly exposed day after day in the columns of *The Times*. The *Gazette* was eagerly read for its dispatches, but it could not compare with the independent newspaper serviced by its own correspondents and directed by an Editor conscious of his duty towards the public.

The Times brought down Aberdeen's Government, obtained the dismissal of the Commander-in-Chief, rescued "the remnant of an army" and beat to its knees "the cold shade of aristocracy". To crown all on January 17 1856 the paper printed the news of Russian capitulation before the Prime Minister had received the official dispatch.† Politicians complained that the country was ruled by a newspaper, that decisions of government became impossible if they had to be ratified by *The Times*. It was a dangerous eminence not again to be achieved. That it could have been held was proof that no Government newspaper was needed "to get facts right", that a government-sponsored newspaper could not compete with a responsible independent journal.

During these years so momentous for journalism Watts died and was succeeded as Editor, Manager and Publisher by Thomas L. Behan, appointed by the Foreign Office on October 1 1854 at a salary of £600, rising to £800 by steps of £25.‡ McCulloch had no more to report to the Treasury than the theft of £16 from the *Gazette* office—for which he held Behan responsible since he found the money had not been kept in proper

*In a rudimentary form: full open competition was not introduced until 1870.

†*The History of "The Times"* (1939), iii, 191.

‡Stationery Office Authority Book.

security. Financially he was dissatisfied only with the lowered selling price, by which the Exchequer failed to reap the benefit of increased wartime sales.

Company Law

The number of advertisements continued to grow: 26,247 in 1857. Issues seldom contained fewer than 24 pages, including perhaps 18 columns of advertising under Acts regulating partnership and insolvency. The Patent Law Amendment Act passed in 1852 produced a crop of paid insertions.*

As the ancient editorial primacy conferred by prerogative power flickered out Parliament redressed the balance by calling into existence new advertising under requirements of statutory publicity. In 1855 the principle of limited liability that was to transform business not only in Britain but throughout the world was first recognized in the Act of that year and in the following year the principle of giving information to the investing public was appended. Then came legislation on bankruptcy, company liquidation and dissolution of partnerships.† It continued the concept behind the insolvent debtors Acts of the last century: that the businessman losing money must publicize the fact: the *Gazette* was to be his pillory. This kind of provision brought much advertising to its pages for during the years 1875–83 about 20 % of companies registered went bankrupt within five years of formation.‡

Before new legislation affecting the *Gazette* had reached its peak McCulloch died on November 11 1864. He was succeeded by William Rathbone Greg, who early in life had thrown up a business career for political journalism. The radical philosophers of his native Lancashire had influenced him but a

*15 and 16 Vict. c. 83.

†The Limited Liability Act, 18 and 19 Vict. c. 133; The Joint Stock Companies Act, 19 and 20 Vict. c. 47.

‡J. H. Clapham: *An Economic History of Modern Britain* (Cambridge 1938), iii, 202.

gift for logical writing, a gentleness of character and universal philanthropy endeared him to all and Palmerston, then Prime Minister, gave him financial security by appointing him to the Comptrollership of the Stationery Office. This post for such appointments was becoming known as "the deanery of the civil service".

"The Chief Work . . . of the Gazette *Office"*

Although Greg scrupulously refrained from interference with the editorial side of the *Gazette* he had a low opinion of Behan's occupation: it required no talent, it was not even full-time. When the Editor asked for a rise Greg refused it and further justified his action to the Treasury: the receipt, calculation, acceptance and recording of payment for advertisements was "*the* work—the chief work—almost the only material and pressing work, except paying the money into the Bank—of the *Gazette* office". By 1866 the number of advertisements had risen to 41,049. Like his predecessor he condemned the lowered selling price: "nor do I imagine that a single additional copy has been sold in consequence of the reduction. No one buys the *Gazette* for amusement, or as pleasant reading. Those who *must* have it, care little or nothing whether they pay 1s. or 2s. 8d. for it".*

*Greg to George Hamilton, December 14 1867, S.O. Letterbooks.

Chapter IX 1868–1910

Treasury Intervention

Gladstone, having formed his first administration in 1868, appointed a monumental commission of enquiry into public accounts that stripped the last vestiges of eighteenth-century confusion of public and private monies from Government bookkeeping. George Hamilton, Auditor of the Civil List and Permanent Secretary of the Treasury—a then new title replacing that of Assistant Secretary—chaired a committee, Greg sitting with Arthur Helps, Clerk of the Privy Council, that in January 1869 discussed the future of the *Gazette*. Although advertisements were to the forefront, editorial contents were not neglected. The use of the *Gazette* when Parliament was not sitting to give publicity to information that would otherwise have been conveyed by a question and answer in either House was approved, and the responsibility for supplying the information was laid on ministers and departmental heads.* The committee was not in favour of radical change on the model of the French official paper, the *Moniteur*, which contained leading articles presenting and expounding Government policy. The "perfect neutrality" of the *Gazette* was to be preserved.†

The Committee on Public Accounts was in the throes of its investigation when Behan died on August 30 1869. He left, so Greg discovered, in the St James's Square branch of the London

*Of the departments approached to approve this suggestion only the Admiralty considered it might do more harm than good.

†The Home Office copy of the Report, sent by the Treasury on March 6 1869, is H.O. 45 OS 8292 (1).

and Westminster Bank £129 18s. of public money in an account opened jointly with a clerk from the *Gazette* office. It represented unclaimed overpayments for insertions: denied an official rise Behan had taken his own increment. This small scandal highlighted the need for Treasury intervention.

The three-man committee had already considered the post of Superintendent. "With regard to the *Gazette* itself," they reported, "however cumbersome and apparently overloaded with official advertisements, it is an important publication; and although the duties of the Superintendent cannot be regarded as heavy, yet he has considerable responsibility connected with a publication which contains official notifications, many of them having the character of legal evidence. . . . He has also occasionally to attend out of office hours, and to see to the proper insertion of Orders in Council and public dispatches, as well as to superintend the receipt, and provide for the temporary custody of considerable sums of money."

On Behan's death the opportunity was taken to request the Home and Foreign Secretaries to renounce their right of alternate appointment of Editor, the sole vestige of the once intimate and lucrative connection. It was thus the Treasury that on October 5 1869 appointed Thomas Walker, a former Editor of the *Daily News*, to be Editor, Manager and Publisher of the *Gazette*, the Stationery Office remaining responsible for the printing arrangement with Harrisons and for scrutiny of the accounts.*

Had the three-man committee been able to ensure that ministers made full use of the *Gazette* as a medium of giving "information to the public", the official journal might have been revitalized. A greater franchise had however been won too late. The Editor of an independent journal must—to be a full

*Stationery Office Authority Book by Treasury letter of October 6 1869. Walker's salary was the same as Behan's, £600–800 by £25. The three-man committee had not recommended a reduction in view of the responsibility for accuracy and honesty.

Editor—anticipate news and have sources to enable him to confirm what is released officially or unofficially to him. Walker as *Gazette* writer was entirely dependent on ministers, first to make the decision to release news and secondly to decide on its formulation. Gladstone himself, although he did not neglect the Press, was aridly official, and he laid an embargo on the communication of news by civil servants: the Chief Whip informed the Editor of *The Times* in December 1868: "I have learnt that I can't give you NEWS!!"* With such views ruling Walker had a dusty prospect.

Greg had his own ordeal in the summer of 1873 when he was summoned before a select committee on purchases by public departments. It was disturbed to learn that he was seldom in the Office for more than three or four hours a day and often less. Hot for certainties the committee found none in him; although they should have been cheered by the profit of £21,000 a year for the *Gazette*. Their recommendation was "that when a vacancy occurred, provision should be made for uniting the control of the Stationery department with the management of the *Gazette* by the appointment of a man possessing the requisite knowledge of stationery and printing".

Thomas Digby Pigott

Although Gladstone went out of office in 1874 the Treasury kept Greg and the *Gazette* on a close rein for four years, during which the profit rose to £27,000. Greg, over 65, resigned in 1877. Instead of the candidate for whom the committee had indicated its preference, Beaconsfield, then Prime Minister, appointed Thomas Digby Pigott, who had entered the War Office in 1859 as a temporary clerk. Established in the following year, he had since been private secretary to a succession of ministers. No one claimed he had "the requisite knowledge of stationery and printing". His starting salary was cut from £1,200 to £1,000, the

*The History of "The Times" (1939), iii, 409.

title was changed from Comptroller, which smacked of the Household and white staff, to Controller, and he was warned that he might have to undertake the superintendence of the *Gazette* as an extra but unpaid duty.

The Commons resented the slight to the Committee of 1873 as well as to qualified senior staff at the Stationery Office. It seemed as if patronage were again rearing its ugly head, the more so since Pigott's father had once been rector of Beaconsfield's home parish. A motion of censure was carried by four votes on July 16 1877 and Pigott tendered his resignation. Defence being offered a trifle unconvincingly in the House of Lords by the Prime Minister and in the Commons by a poorly briefed Chancellor of the Exchequer (Northcote), the censure was after long debate withdrawn.* Pigott began his new job painfully aware that his predecessor offered no model for conduct and that his was a department over which both Commons and Treasury watched with lidless eyes.

The Editor Dropped

So envigilated Pigott became an apostle of economy and was to claim in 1890 that "the cost of a first-class battleship, complete with its armament, with an attendant flotilla of half a dozen gunboats, has during the last 10 years been saved, without inconvenience to the public, on Government printing and stationery". One of the savings in which he took pride was in the *Gazette*. At the time when he was bestowing potential armament upon the Navy the contract with Harrisons was due for renewal. In January 1890 the Controller sat with Treasury officials in a small committee to consider whether the time had not come for a reorganization. From their sessions emerged the decision, apparently taken without a qualm, to drop the office of Superintendent. All was to be done by the printer under the authority of the Stationery Office. Under the new contract

*Hansard, ccxxxv, pp. 1330, 1477 and 1690, July 16, 19 and 20.

Harrisons were to pay £800 a year for the privilege and were to sell the *Gazette* at fixed prices, and the fees were to be paid into the Exchequer. Otherwise the *Gazette* was transferred, lock, stock and barrel, to the hinterland of the printing house in St Martin's Lane and one of the Harrison family undertook the editing.

In some respects a decision of this nature was long overdue. At the end of the eighteenth century the Secretaries had regarded the job of *Gazette* writer as a reward of good service and diligence, and once the hunt for sinecures was up it was certain to be questioned. The Treasury as re-created by Gladstone was an all-powerful department, inflexibly conscious of its responsibility for public money. The venality of Rose was abhorrent to the heirs of Trevelyan.

Then, even Greg in 1870 had declared of the *Edinburgh Gazette*: "there is no need whatever of an Editor."* For that *Gazette* and its running mate of Dublin other seemingly satisfactory arrangements had been made. The turn of the *London Gazette* had come. On August 1 1889 Walker retired on pension and the clerical staff of the *Gazette* were absorbed into the Stationery Office.†

Statutory Publicity

In the second half of the nineteenth century, while the Treasury was preoccupied with collecting fees and cutting costs, the *Gazette* was enjoying something of a golden age as a medium of statutory publicity. Under the Documentary Evidence Act of 1868‡, for instance, it was prima facie evidence of Proclamations, Orders in Council and certain other regulations. In theory the Crown's journal was appropriately linked with executive functions of the Crown, although in practice by 1868 government

*Greg, writing on November 3 1870, on the death of Laurie, a Scots Watts who was Publisher, Editor and Printer of the *Edinburgh Gazette* (S.O. letterbooks).

†Stationery Office Authority Book 1880–1910, July 29 1889.

‡31 and 32 Victoria c. 37.

by proclamation was restricted to formal occasions and Orders in Council increasingly originated with the Cabinet, a body without authority to make Orders but having often a dual membership with the Privy Council which had.*

The documents in the 1868 Act were even then being overtaken by statutory instruments. The pressure of work on a reformed Parliament led to Acts framed in general terms that delegated the detailed legislation to subordinate institutions or officials. The Rules Publication Act of 1893 brought such legislation into the sphere of the *Gazette* by providing that statutory rules and orders should be published there 40 days before coming into operation. This procedure could have kept the *Gazette* abreast of changing constitutional developments but much material was to slip through. There were many instruments not covered by the provision, nor did it include such rules and orders as under the parent statute were to be laid before the House for a specified period.†

Nevertheless, legislative attention enhanced the prestige of the *Gazette* elsewhere than in solicitors' offices, and the decision to drop the pilot had perhaps not been well-timed. In other newspaper offices, where it was more familiar than to the general public, and where, since the repeal of the stamp Act, an Editor had grown into a lord of creation, the staffing of the official newspaper seemed comic, certainly undignified. In January 1895 the *Gazette*, by the sort of slip to which Delafaye had been prone, described in a Foreign Office item the Foreign Secretary as Earl of Kimberley instead of Earl Kimberley. The *Daily News*, Walker's former paper, seized on the error to bring the dropping

*The regulation of the modern civil service after 1855 was amost entirely laid down by Orders in Council.

†56 and 57 Vict. c. 66. D. L. Keir, *The Constitutional History of Modern Britain 1485–1951* (1953). The contents of the *Gazette* were so increased by statutory insertions that 64-page issues were normal. By the end of the century all the brilliance of Clarke's typography had been lost and the grey effect that was fashionable in the last decades of Victoria's reign was relieved only by the tabular settings then extravagantly employed.

86

of the *Gazette* Editor to public notice: "A newspaper, even an
official newspaper, without an Editor is ridiculous. . . . A foolish
and cheeseparing economy suggested the abolition of the
Editor. . . . The idea of leaving the official journal without a head
can only be described as grotesque." *Vanity Fair* added its
hap'orth: "The *Gazette* indeed is in many ways a most
important publication. No man of business would leave even a
second-rate *Tit-Bits* to the editing of its printer and its
advertisers; but Government Departments, of course, are not
men of business."*

For the newspapers of Fleet Street the *Gazette* was a
permissible dog to be eaten since it could not eat them, but there
was some justice in the mockery. Greg had written to Gladstone
in 1870 that "the notion of *farming* out any branch of the Public
Revenue is not likely to be entertained nowadays. . . . Such is not
the fashion in which a responsible Government publication could
be permitted to be conducted."† Pigott in 1889 believed that his
retention of nominal authority and certain restrictions on the
printer's freedom to accept advertisements safeguarded the
advertisement columns from the danger his predecessor had
feared, the invasion by those seeking publicity for its own sake.
He had ignored the status of the *Gazette*, its position in the
hierarchy of the Press as well as in the Civil Service. And not
only was his New Establishment a degradation and not only did
the rewards fall short of those expected, but the tide of evolution
within the Stationery Office was to make farming an exploded
system.

Within a few years of Pigott's retirement in 1905 at the age of
65 his sucessor Sir Frederick Atterbury had collected the printing
and publishing of the *Votes and Proceedings* and of the Commons'
Journals and in 1909 the printing and publishing of the *Debates*,

*S.O. Papers, 12.3.L9A.95, clippings of the *Daily News* for January 3 1895 and
Vanity Fair for January 12.

†Greg to Gladstone, October 27 1870.

known as Hansard. Patents fell like autumn leaves and the arrangements that McCulloch had so detested were transformed into contracts from which the public could only benefit although as yet the Stationery Office could not undertake its own printing.

The "New Establishment" of 1910

It was unfitting that the *Gazette* should be the sheep outside the fold and when the current contract with Harrisons was due to fall in in 1910 remedial action was taken. Under the new terms, which were for printing only at a discount of 30%, the editing and receipt of advertisements were to take place at a *London Gazette* Office at 7 Princes Street, Westminster, under a Superintendent seconded from the Stationery Office. It was expected that his work would require two hours a day—Greg had often spent only two hours on the entire work of his department— and William Codling therefore retained his position as private secretary to the Controller, his salary being increased by £50 for the responsibility for the *Gazette* delegated to him by the Controller. Treasury approval of yet another New Establishment was given on July 20 1910 and on November 3 Codling took possession of 7 Princes Street. With the issue of November 8 the *Gazette* became a Stationery Office publication.*

*S.O. Authority Book 1910–23.

Chapter X 1910–65

The Effects of War

When put up to public tender the printing contract had been lost
by Harrisons to Wyman & Sons, printers of a number of
periodicals and proprietors of a chain of bookstalls. The new
arrangement proved financially satisfactory to the Stationery
Office since the average profits for the years 1909–14 were
£29,260. Then for the *Gazette* as for other newspapers came the
pinch. In wartime certain categories of advertising, for instance
bankruptcies, fall away; many of the fees for insertions were
controlled by statutes passed when the purchasing power of the
pound was untouched by a war so consuming of treasure as that
of 1914–18; and the fixed maximum selling price penalized
issues largely and sometimes solely composed of state intelligence.
The printing in full of most of the Orders in Council and
emergency regulations taxed the capacity of the printers. By 1917
they were required to produce as many as 5,000 copies of issues
averaging nearly 100 pages and publishing often took place daily.
Costs of production rose and sharpest of all was the rise of the cost
of the basic material: paper. The post-war accounts were a ravaged
battlefield: the profits for 1919–20 were only £382 and the
oracles of the Stationery Office forecast leaner years ahead.

In 1919 Codling became Controller. Before the war he had
come into contact with the *Gazette* at a time when the Stationery
Office began to take pride in its antiquity.* It was Codling who
had selected the historic issues that were sent to several national

*No anniversary had been celebrated in 1865.

and international exhibitions although he was not a scholarly man. Bargaining and technical organization were more congenial to him and from the beginning of a small firm in Hare Street, taken over in 1917, he was to assemble an array of printing machinery and craftsmen that would make the Stationery Office a colossus among the country's printing houses. In 1919 he secured as Deputy Controller Norman Gibbs Scorgie, a Cambridge man, trained as a barrister, who quit the Army to enter the Civil Service at the end of 1918 and who for two decades was to work with Codling in a successful partnership of men of widely differing talents. Words sprang to Scorgie, tools of logical or persuasive argument and marshalled fact, more vividly phrased than the conventional style of Civil Service memoranda.

On Scorgie, with his legal training, fell the labour of adjusting the advertisement charges of the *Gazette* to restore the balance of revenue. The calculation and interrelation of rates is one of the most exacting tasks of newspaper management: too much, too little, are equally pregnant with disaster. The *Gazette* presented a simpler pattern than other newspapers but even so mistakes had been made in the past. Scorgie's hands were tied in so far as legislation was required to amend statutory fees, and his powers of analysis and calculation were extended on the range that could without delay be changed.

Other economies received Treasury approval but the departments affected reacted with varying degrees of enthusiasm. Departmental pride sometimes fostered departmental jealousies and the older foundations with their own way of doing things resented criticism of time-honoured methods. What might seem like dictation from the Treasury was received askance by the rest of the Civil Service. Scorgie had patiently to explain and rehearse what was needed to departments and to extraneous bodies, the Friendly Societies, the Law Society and other institutions associated with the *Gazette*.

The Stationery Office begins to Print

In June 1920 Wymans secured a new contract at a premium of 30%. One of the competing tenders had for the first time come from the Stationery Office but its costing was handicapped by heavy capital outlay at Hare Street, which was re-equipped to print Hansard from February 1920, and at the Harrow Printing Works, where in the same year the plant was installed to print the London Telephone Directory. Prices were abnormally high in the trade after the war but Codling was convinced that stabilization would be reached within a few years. Meanwhile he had to look to Scorgie to effect the compensating savings. The year 1920 saw the worst financial crisis the *Gazette* had faced.

The situation changed more rapidly than the Controller could have expected. In March 1923 a strike in the Paper Workers Union affected the warehousing of the *Gazette* and Wymans were unable to complete publication between March 27 and April 20. The jeopardy in which the official journal was placed strengthened the Controller's resolve to use the proviso in the contract that enabled either side to end it in June 1923, and he then transferred the *Gazette* to Hare Street without putting up a contract to public tender.

For this highhanded action he was criticized in the trade and questions were asked in Parliament, but he held that the necessity to ensure continuity of the *Gazette* overrode all other considerations. Thus after June 1923 the official journal passed into the keeping of the Stationery Office. Within two years the combined efforts of Codling and Scorgie and a healthier situation in the trade were visible in rising profits and once again the *Gazette* was financially secure.

Suggestions for its enlargement, editorial reorganization, rationalization and popularization did not abate. One of the most interesting was that proposed in 1923 by a former Editor of the *Pall Mall Gazette*, D. M. Sutherland, who, alarmed at the abbreviated reports of Parliament printed in the low-price newspapers, pressed for an amalgamation of the *Gazette* with Hansard. On technical grounds it was rejected. Hansard was printed late at night for early morning delivery to members throughout the five months of the year that Parliament was in session. The *Gazette* was day work for afternoon publication twice weekly throughout the year. They could no more be profitably combined than chalk and cheese.

The Controller did not regard it as his duty to lay down what the *Gazette* should or should not contain. Nor was any defence by himself and Scorgie of its integrity based on sentimental or antiquarian grounds. They did not grow dewy-eyed at the reflection that it was the oldest newspaper in the country. To them, as to McCulloch, financial health was paramount. Although the accounts of the *Gazette* were separate it was the responsibility of a department which was accustomed to calculate profit and loss. The wheel set in motion by the nineteenth-century radicals was turning fast: the duty of giving information to the public, in the form of matured research or analysis to provide a basis for decision, was being accepted in the Civil Service. Departments offered catalogues, statistical tables, interim and final reports; but rarely best-sellers. So successful was the Stationery Office in balancing its books that in 1961, after years of rising costs within the trade, the then Controller, Sir John Simpson, could claim that "Government publishing, except for copies used for official purposes, is conducted without any cost to the State".

McCulloch however had had no part in editorial matters and had abstained from interference or comment. After 1910 the Stationery Office had enlarged responsibility and Scorgie did not confine himself to a mercenary assessment of the value of the *Gazette*. Himself a barrister he knew that to the legal world it was "a depository of valuable working material". Although in the cause of economy he made repeated efforts to prune the state intelligence, he never gainsaid the duty of the *Gazette* to find room for items that would be given publicity nowhere else. In such contents lay its irreplaceable value, not so much directly to the general public as to the Press. As in the seventeenth century the *Gazette* was still source material for other newspapers.

The "Prime Source" of State Intelligence

He did not overvalue the "authority" under which it was published, knowing that it had been shredded away in the course of constitutional change: an "authority" so old, he once remarked, "that no one today has any real authority" and the *Gazette* "runs as it were on the wound up tradition of centuries". He was ready to admit the insignificance, numerically, of the circulation; he confessed that "under the conditions in which it must be compiled it necessarily suffers for want of effective sub-editing". But he was positive that "it would be unwise to underrate the importance of the *Gazette*. . . . It must always remain the prime source of 'State intelligence' ".*

This was the function that was guarded by the Controller and his Deputy. In May 1926 they had to do battle for the principle. During the General Strike, when the publication of other newspapers ceased,† the Government of the day resolved to put out its own newspaper under the title of the *London Gazette*. This the Stationery Office resisted: such an appropriation of the prestige of the official journal violated that "perfect neutrality" that Harley, Walpole, Bute, Rose, Palmerston and other party-allied statesmen had respected, that during more than two centuries had been the distinction of the *London Gazette*. They protested against the sacrifice of that long-established identity for a passing advantage, and they won: the Coalition Government's paper was christened the *British Gazette*.

This defence was not lightly undertaken for it was the

*The quotations are taken from letters written by Scorgie to H. E. C. Gatliff at the Treasury on October 5 1938 and to Lt. Col. Sir Arnold Wilson on July 14 1937.

†Only *The Times* was able to print an emergency edition daily in London.

Chancellor of the Exchequer, Winston Churchill, who led the
demand for the title and the Stationery Office is directly
responsible to the Chancellor. Controller and Deputy Controller
skirted mutiny. But to them their ground was clear: the
separation of the permanent Civil Service of the Crown from the
Government of ministers responsible to Parliament.

The Modern Role of the Gazette

The situation was for the *Gazette* a crystallization of the years of
national struggle to keep Crown and Civil Service out of politics.
It reflected the tensions familiar to politicians since the Commons
cried out against the placemen of Queen Anne and condemned
the patronage of George III. The *Courant*, the *Briton*, the *True
Briton* and many other captive papers had expired, Rose's *Sun* had
set. The *Gazette* outlived them all, not because it was ably
conducted or well written or inclusive, but because it allied to
the authority of the Crown that ideal neutrality that resides with
the Crown. Ministers come and go as opinions in the backstreets
and the shires change: the Crown is always served. Often
neglected, sometimes despised, several times newly established,
never throughout a career of three hundred years requiring
subsidy, the *Gazette* continues to appear, not by accident, not by
allowance or sentiment, but because it fulfills a function
indispensable under the established constitution of the country.

As Scorgie once wrote: "The Stationery Office is mainly a
trustee of tradition. Punctually we publish on Tuesdays and
Fridays. We modernize the type and make-up slowly and so
imperceptibly that no one is moved to protest.* Dutifully we
publish any notice which the Mother of Parliaments has enacted
shall be published in the *Gazette*. Tactfully we try to mould it
into reasonable form. Against whom a mandamus would lie if it

*On August 19 1958 the present text type and heading style were introduced, and
the traditional "Numb." was superseded by "No." The page size was unaltered at
12 × 7½ in.

were not so published I doubt if the Attorney General could tell you. Vigorously we resist the thrusting publicity agents who wish to use the advertisement columns of the *Gazette* for new forms of publicity, with usually no Treasury or Minister behind us and nothing but 'It is unauthorized and it is unsuitable' as our last ditch."

Since the *Gazette* ceased to be a source of private emolument there has been continual pressure for it to be adapted, expanded, modernized. Meanwhile other newspapers have been adapted, expanded and modernized admirably to fulfill the function of the unofficial Press: to maintain eternal vigilance on the actions and intentions of Government. The *Gazette* has changed slowly, as Crown and constitution and Civil Service have changed: it has kept pace with those institutions of which it is the organ. Reformers jeer at its anomalies, but they harm no one and are relics of ancient pride and state. It is itself an anomaly. To quote once more the words of the Deputy Controller in whose charge the *Gazette* was confided: "If you turn a powerful Committee on to such an institution nowadays it could not survive. This great executive instrument of the Privy Council, which has long outlived all real executive authority of the Council itself, could not stand the buffeting zeal of reformers beating on its ancient trunk when its roots are anchored only in a soil that has crumbled to dust."

That dust is honoured: the dust of discarded patterns of a constitution of checks and balances responding to the national will. Such striving cannot cease and to chronicle future change is the responsibility of the official journal of fact and record: the *London Gazette* celebrating its three hundredth birthday on November 16 1965.

Dmd. 120684 K20   S.O. Code No. 70–887*